COLOR
HARMONY
for the web

ROCKPORT

First published in the United States of America by
Rockport Publishers, Inc.
33 Commercial Street
Gloucester, Massachusetts 01930-5089
Telephone: (978) 282-9590
Facsimile: (978) 283-2742
www.rockpub.com

ISBN 1-56496-603-8

10 9 8 7 6 5 4 3 2

Layout: SYP Design & Production
www.sypdesign.com
Cover Design: Francesco Jost
Front cover image design, clockwise from top
left: CO2 Media; Campeau Communications;
Natalie Tzobanakis; Dept. of Computer Graphic
Design; twenty2product; François Chalet.
Back cover image design, clockwise from top left:
Epoxy; Fast Lane Studios; Juxt Interactive.

Printed in China.

COLOR
HARMONY
for the web

A GUIDEBOOK TO CREATE COLOR COMBINATIONS FOR WEB SITE DESIGN

Cailin Boyle

Acknowledgments

Thank you to the designers and creative
directors who were so open about their
work. Your enthusiasm, interest, and
dedication made this a wonderfully
enlightening project. Thanks especially
to Mark Wyman for his support and
assistance. Special thanks to Ann Fox for
doing an outstanding job of keeping me
on track. And to you for reading this,
I hope you enjoy the book.

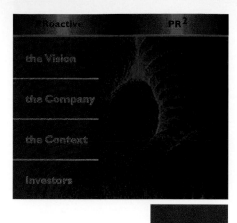

Contents

Introduction 6

Welcome to Color 8

Why Is Color Important? 10

The Color Wheel 14

Color on the Web 16

CMYK Process Color 20

Aspects of Color 22

Nostalgic 26

Multicultural 34

Fresh 42

Earthy 50

Lively 58

Romantic 66

Energetic 74

Calming 82

Classic 90

Bold 98

Subdued 106

Refreshing 114

Aggressive 122

Friendly 130

Vibrant 138

Professional 146

Elegant 154

Welcoming 162

Going Forward 170

Color Conversion Chart 175

Color Swatches 177

Credits 189

Directory 191

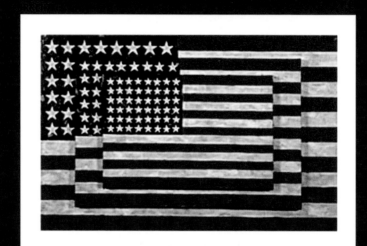

THE AMERICAN CENTURY,

PART 2; ART & CULTURE 1950–2000

ORGANIZED BY THE WHITNEY MUSEUM OF AMERICA
ART AND PRESENTED BY INTEL CORPORATION

4.0+ browser required

Introduction

Color enters every part of our life.

When creating good design, creatives must fully understand both the range of color available and its power to convey feelings. The relation of color to mood is so ingrained that it is like a trigger response. We are calmed by the color of the sky on a sunny day. Grass green brings a feeling of freshness to whatever it touches. Sunshine yellow makes us feel happier. How we relate to color is intrinsic and, with few exceptions, cross-cultural.

Within each range of color are tints or hues that move, for example, from bright, vibrant, pulsating red to soft, pale, quiet pink. Creating exciting and effective design is, in large part, about understanding the subtleties and power of color and how it can work for you—and sometimes against you.

An understanding of color and how it works is critical to developing powerful web design. This means appreciating the limits of this web medium and how best to take advantage of its offerings.

The web, as a means of communication, is instantaneous, changeable, and borderless. A design posted in San Francisco is viewed the same day in Shanghai. An event in Sydney can be webcast and seen live in Santiago. With these opportunities comes the challenge: Never has design needed to be so compelling and universal.

Web design has traditionally been created in industrial nations, yet less developed nations now have wide accessibility to the web also. Designers can come from anywhere on the planet, from the smallest villages in the most remote areas to the towers of design in the capital cities. Web sites can be launched in tiny towns and viewed in corporate headquarters. With the growing range of the web, both its design and its audience expand daily. As designers can no longer tightly identify their market, they must use all the elements available to them to effectively communicate with this potentially universal audience.

Color Harmony for the Web is for designers, web artists, and those looking to use the web to expand their reach. We begin with background information about color and its psychological effects, the demographic palette, trends in color, and web-specific concerns. Then we explore how designers have successfully solved various communication challenges through their design and the use of color.

We also include a color chart of the 216 web-safe colors. This chart allows designers to reference the available colors and their Hex code equivalents. The site examples include large corporate and e-commerce sites as well as small sites promoting local bands; this broad range allows comparison of successful designs and their elements.

Whether you're new to web design, a seasoned webmaster, or someone looking to better understand what makes for good web design, *Color Harmony for the Web* will help you explore the power of color in this new medium and how to use it effectively.

dive into total entertainment

| FO-DESK | CHAT | GAMES | T - E - N |
| | E-MAIL | USENET | ARCHIVES |

reduce, re-use, recycle

A REASONED SEQUENCE:
GOING TO, ARRIVING AT, LEAVING WITH

mail   page   back

Welcome to Color

Design on the web has grown with its use. In 1992 there were only about 50 web sites. The latest statistics track the number of web sites at 3.6 million, with additional sites coming online at a rate of 4,400 per day! Whether or not you love the web, there's no denying its growing importance: The U.S. Department of Commerce's Census Bureau recently released its first set of e-commerce numbers, reporting that online retail sales were $5.3 billion for the fourth quarter of 1999.

The number of actual web pages has also reached epidemic proportions. NEC Research estimates that there are around 1.5 billion web pages, with the number expected to reach 8 billion in the year 2002, exceeding the world's population.

The number of potential web sites also continues to grow. Registrar Network Solutions registered 4.7 million new domain names in 1999. That's more than double their registrations in 1998, for a total of about 8.1 million registered names.

However, amid this breadth of choice, research indicates that 80 percent of users only visit 15,000 sites, or just 0.4 percent of all pages available. Therefore to keep and attract attention, web sites need to focus their efforts. Along with effective site architecture and content, the design and use of color are key to attracting and branding a site, building mindshare with users and the number of all-important return visitors.

In this book we'll explore the aspects of color, from its psychological effects to its limitations when designing for the web. We'll also review several web sites that successfully use color, and we'll explore why the colors work and what inspired the creative directors and designers when creating the site.

SUMATRA COFFEE
MANDHELING
WHOLE BEAN COFFEE
NET WT. 1 LB. (453g)

KENYA AA PLUS
WHOLE BEAN COFFEE
NET WT. 1 LB. (453g)

COSTA RICA COFFEE
TARRAZU
WHOLE BEAN COFFEE
NET WT. 1 LB. (453g)

JAMAICA COFFEE
BLUE MOUNTAIN BLEND
WHOLE BEAN COFFEE
NET WT. 1 LB. (453g)

Why Is Color Important?

Do you ever see red? Feel blue? Become green with envy? We tend to associate certain colors with particular emotions because colors have the power to influence our feelings. They strike a chord deep inside us, and we subconsciously respond to their subtle persuasion.

Color plays a role in every design created. Even black-and-white designs convey meaning through their tones. Designers use colors to ignite certain emotions in their target audiences or facilitate brand recognition. Who doesn't recognize the bright orange of the Tide box or the signature red of Coca-Cola? Colors should reflect the image or the message you're sending as you aim for a particular response from the target audience.

The first step in understanding color is knowing how colors influence you in relation to how colors influence your audience. Put colors in their proper perspective. Some colors, for example, may be popular but have negative connotations. We all have personal associations with color; it's easy to put our own prejudices on color. Designers must get beyond cultural background and negative feelings to explore the full range of colors available to them. As children, we may be taught or told certain things about color, such as that orange is cheap or tacky, or that it's not an upscale color. But look at designers like Versace. They're using more orange. You may have this little voice in your head saying "I can't use this." However it's in the context of usage, how and where, that determines what works. So much of your own opinion goes into each color choice. It's important to get beyond personal reactions and responses to properly explore color options.

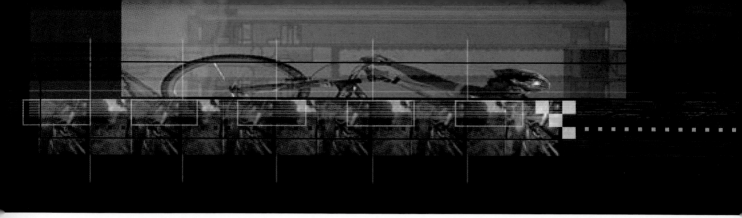

Demographic palette

Part of the challenge in color selection is that different audiences respond differently to particular colors—and the trends are always shifting. On some level, the demographic color palette has been reversed. For example, the old-school approach to designing for children called for generous use of primary colors—the bright colors to which kids are thought to respond. Think of PlaySkool and Fisher Price equipment: reds and yellows and blues. Yet, color palettes for older kids are much more sophisticated. Because older kids and adolescents tend to aspire to the age group above them, today's pre-teens prefer the darker colors favored by Generations X and Y. They respond to black, muddied browns and grays interspersed with flashes of bright color.

Meanwhile, the elderly population is experiencing an opposite reaction to color. Traditionally thought to favor softer, mellow tones, today's seniors are leading more active, involved lives in society: Their tastes and wardrobes reflect this with brighter colors. Designers need to understand the demographic trends when developing images for age-specific groups. Remember, seniors are not sitting at home knitting. Go out. See how active they are and what colors they're wearing. Incorporate these colors into your designs. Reflect their lives in your choice of color.

Popularity shifts

The popularity of colors tends to intensify and fade, and designers should always be aware of what colors are "in" and what colors are not. To discover which colors are popular, we only need to look around us and see what is prevalent. Remember to look outside your field. If you're a graphic designer, look at the world of fashion or Hollywood. Colors and their popularity come from places other than graphic design. Keep an eye out for what's popular in other media. Trends in fashion, for example, will often translate into trends in design one or two years later.

To identify which colors may become popular, and coming trends in color, immerse yourself in pop culture— including art and television. Entertainment magazines, for example, reveal which colors are being used to promote new films. If the film becomes popular, then the colors used to promote it will become popular. Fashion is also a great source. It's where you'll see the new colors and color combinations first.

Designers who once complained of restrictions imposed by clients now realize that client attitudes about color have changed. Companies are recognizing the importance of color in marketing. Consider the use of color with the iMac, for example, and other products traditionally in neutral colors, such as cell phones and radios. Previously you had items in either a gray or black. Now these items are available in tortoiseshell, bright reds, and other "fashion" colors.

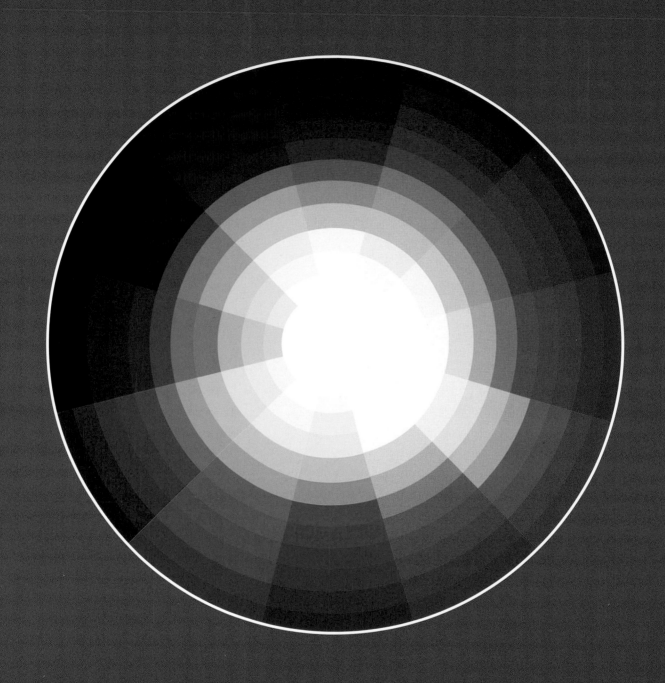

The Color Wheel

The color wheel divides colors into primary, secondary, and tertiary color. The three primary colors are those that aren't made from blends of other colors. They are Red, Blue, Yellow. These colors form an equilateral triangle in the color wheel. Secondary colors are those that come from blending two primary colors: Purple (a blend of red and blue), Green (a blend of blue and yellow), and Orange (a blend of yellow and red). They are also positioned equidistant in the color wheel. Tertiary colors are then a blend of a primary and secondary color.

Looking at the color wheel, we can see the relationship between the colors. The twelve segments of the color wheel are arranged by specific tints and shades. A full level of saturation or brightness means that there is no black, white, or gray added to the color. Adding white to any of the twelve colors results in lighter colors or tints, moving in to the center of the color wheel. For example, pink is a tint of red. Shades are created by adding black or gray to the color, moving to the outer ring of the color wheel. For example, maroon is a shade of red. By seeing the effect of shades and tints and their relation to other colors in the color wheel, we can visualize the balance of colors as we're planning a palette.

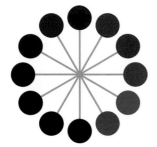

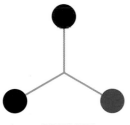

PRIMARY

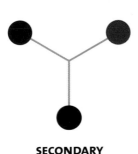

SECONDARY   **TERTIARY**

DigiScents iSmell digital scent technology brings the sense of smell to your computer Send scented holiday and greeting cards, immerse yourself in scented **movies and entertainment, interactive games and music**, sniff before you **buy online**, and **travel to faraway worlds** without leaving your seat. With DigiScents iSmell software and devices you can explore and express yourself in ways you never thought possible. To learn more, read **The DigiScents Story** or watch our **Video**.

Scentware Developers Kit Raises a Stink for over 200 Game Developers!

Smells Like a Fun Time: DigiScents Piques Kids Noses on National Sense of Smell Day.

Race to map human genome: **DoubleTwist, leading biotech company** started by DigiScents' co-founders **Joel Bellenson and Dexster Smith**, first to analyze human genome.

Hot News! DigiScents and Procter & Gamble Form Strategic Alliance.

Sweet!!! DigiScents and eCandy partner to sweeten the online shopping experience.

sign up for our scentware sdk 250 developers (and counting!)

business scents   scentworld   smellorama   shopping scenter   developers   the snortal

company info

join the **revolution** of the **senses!**

Sign up now for **First Whiff**, our exclusive mailing list that will bring you the latest news and promotions. Sign up now for **First Whiff**, our exclusive mailing list that will bring you the latest news and promotions.

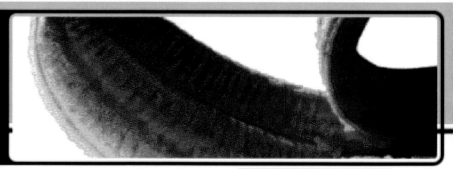

first whiff!

Color on the Web

Text type tips

There are three types of text colors on the web: Text, Links, and Visited links. Each of these elements must work differently with color.

Remember that when designing for the web, the primary goal is information, or content, and therefore the text must be legible. Use a high level of contrast between the text and the background to allow the text to be readable. The most legible color combination is black text on a white background—easy, but not interesting. Be careful reversing the text out of the background, that is, using a light text on a dark background. This strategy may look interesting, but if you don't choose your colors carefully, the reader will struggle to take in the content.

Links usually have a brighter color than the body text. In this way they are easy to identify. They also work to attract the reader, therefore keeping them at the site for a longer period (the objective of the site design,) making the site "stickier"—the adjective used for really effective sites.

You need to signal to the user which links are new and which have been visited. Generally choose a darker color for visited links, allowing the non-visited links to stand out.

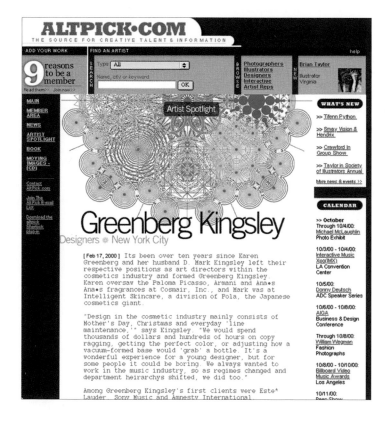

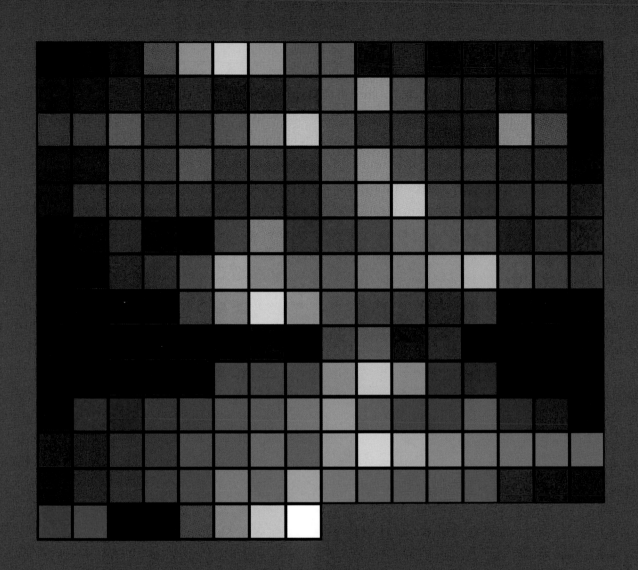

The browser-safe color palette

Images on your color video monitor are created by use of three phosphors, red, green, and blue, which are activated by an electronic beam. You can only see colors on your monitor that fall within the range covered by these three colors. Because of this requirement, colors for the web are specified by their Red, Green, and Blue color values, or RGB. Colors for HTML, hexidecimal numbers, are specified by #RRGGBB. The # sign indicates that it's a color code in HTML. The first two numbers in the RR position reference the red content of the color, the second pair of numbers in the GG position reference the green content, and the third pair of numbers in the BB position reference the blue content of the color.

To make using color on the web even more challenging, realize that most computer monitors can only display 256 colors at once. Yet, with digital technology, designers can create up to 16.7 million colors. Despite a designer's desire to use a certain color, if it won't show up on a user's screen, the color will be shifted or "dithered" and the effect lost. Metallic colors, for example, are popular in print design. Include them in your web design, and metallic silver can appear gray, and that just-right gold may become a bland yellow. The quality of an image depends on the capabilities of the user's hardware and software. To display images, Netscape Navigator and Microsoft Internet Explorer use only the 216 colors that are common to Macintosh and Windows operating systems. These 216 colors have been dubbed the "Browser-Safe Palette."

If a design consists of images created on a 256-color palette, when displayed on a browser using a Browser-Safe Palette, the colors will shift, depending on the browser and the platform. This problem is most noticeable in areas of a design where there are large areas that use a single color. Here there will be a noticeable shift in color, often with less-than-pleasing outcomes. Using a Browser-Safe Palette helps designers achieve predictable results.

STEMS OFFERS A FULL
S, INCLUDING:

loping and manufacturing quality hardware and software to create optimized
systems.

are overwhelmed by the myriad products on the market. And many clients don't
rmed buying decision, GVS can offer you this essential service, recommending and
ture growth path.

mer support team. We offer telephone and on-line support, as well as 7x24 on-site

phisticated workflow. GVS designs and implements accurate color workflows—from
output. With considerable expertise in printing and color processes, GVS technicians
optimized color management and maximum performance from your color output devices.
ring and maintaining a pure color workflow.

tems maintenance plans, customized to your needs. We combine our excellent technical

efficiency

Grande
answers. GVS provides a full range of workflow solution

graphics, print publishing, and Web industries. Every G

exceeds, our customers' primary requirements for cost

upgradability and scalability.

INNOVAT

More than ten years ago
SCSI interface for the A
and development.

Our engineers have wor
systems expertise. This
such as Apple, Hewlet
efficiency you need to

Add to our record of
and service, and you'

storage

GRANDE VITESSE SYSTEMS

UTIONS

t consistently
ative solutions that
design and production
services to large
on its feeding
exacting needs
izi CPU route, fast
RAID storage solution,
roductive prepress

speed

GRANDE VITESSE SYSTEMS DESIGNS,
DEVELOPS, AND IMPLEMENTS:

• Server solutions that enable print spooling, OPI/APR
serving, file sharing, media asset management, automatic
PDF creation, and ftp serving.
• Printing solutions for imagesetters, digital proofers,
CTP, color printers, and large-format printers.
• Storage solutions, including removable media, RAID,
DLT, and jukebox storage systems
• Multi CPU routing (MCR), SWITCH, and network
hub solutions for high-speed data transmission
• Workstation solutions for Macintosh, Windows, NT,
UNIX, Novell, and Scitex systems

1.800.794.4622
www.gvsnet.com

© 1998 Grande Vitesse Systems, GVS, Metropolis, and Norvadis are trademarks of Grande Vitesse
Systems. Macintosh is a trademark of Apple Computer, Inc. All other trademarks and registered
trademarks are property of their respective owners.

GVS

For more
that enab
to large
exacting
network

GRANDE VITESSE SYSTEMS DESIGNS, DEVELO

• Server solutions that
serving, file sharing,
PDF creation, and ftp
• Printing solutions fo
CTP, color printers, a
• Storage solutions, i
DLT, and jukebox st
• Multi CPU routing
hub solutions for h
• Workstation soluti
UNIX, Novell, and

GRANDE VITESSE SYSTEMS

PORT/LINK
LED
0 1 2 3

intelligence

CMYK Process Color

CMYK is the standard model used in offset printing for full-color documents. In the CMYK model, all tones are described as a mixture of these four process pigments: Cyan [C], Magenta [M], Yellow [Y], Black [K].

The CMYK palette offers a wide range of colors. To specify a process color, you specify a percentage value for each of the four colors. A nice red, for example, would be 0% C, 100% M, 40% Y, and 0% K. If, however, you'd rather have orange, you would decrease the magenta and increase the yellow: 0% C, 50% M, 100% Y, and 0% K.

The CMYK model is unique in that it works by subtractive, reflective color rather than the additive, radiant color system used by RGB color. Radiant color is produced by the energy radiated from a luminous object such as a cathode-ray tube or a light-emitting diode, hence the color used on the web. RGB is called additive because a color becomes lighter as higher levels of red, green, and blue light are added.

Reflective color, by contrast, represents energy that is not absorbed by a substance such as ink or paint. Pigments and CMYK color work the way color does in nature, according to the subtractive color model. Sunlight contains every visible color. When sunlight is projected onto an object, that object absorbs, or subtracts, some of the light and reflects the remainder. The reflected light is the visible color. For example, a tulip is bright red because it absorbs all non-red from the light spectrum.

CMYK is important to web designers because of the recent repurposing trend. While web color is typically specified in the RGB formula, good web design may need to be converted to CMYK to continue branding in print media, or printed material may form the basis of web design. As the importance of the web for branding and messaging expands, the web-based RGB palette and the print-based CMYK palette must produce colors that match. To this end, many software programs have conversion features that allow RGB colors to be converted to the process colors of the CMYK palette.

Aspects of Color

Historical fluctuations

History shows that each decade has been dominated by color groups synonymous with that time period. The 1950s were pinks. Innocent pastels dominated everything from lipstick to cars. The turbulent '60s brought a period of organized defiance, a freedom to experiment, and a redefinition of fashion. The British Invasion, Twiggy, and the Mod movement—so well captured in the *Austin Powers* movies—reshaped our cultural identity and gave artists the courage to create psychedelic swirls and pop-art prints. Yellows and oranges made famous by Andy Warhol were everywhere. A return to the earth tones in the '70s popularized avocado green, gold, and rust in everything from kitchen decor to clothing. These browns and rusts yielded to the shiny pinks and purples ushered in by the disco era. The extravagant '80s, billed as the Color Conscious Decade, began with glitter and gold and then moved toward powerful red and corporate navy, with muted mauves, grays, and teals.

The 1990s kicked off with neutral tones, predominantly in the green family.

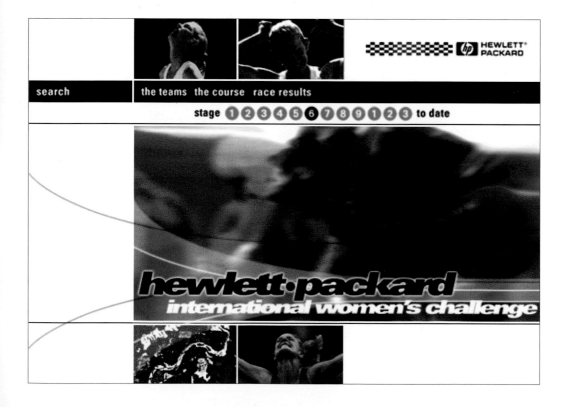

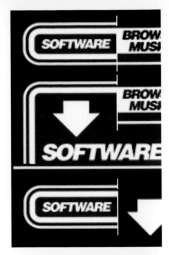

Neutrals like gray, khaki, and navy were popular. The 1990s are best known for the "colored neutrals," soft yellows, yellow-greens, and corals. Tints of pinkish and peach were equally prevalent. Gray took on a lavender or bluish hue. Red was heightened as a tint. Eventually these tints will evolve into the next hot colors. Currently gray, often with a blue cast, is the leading neutral color, while blue-lavender has gained status as the top fashion shade. These current blue undertones provide the indication that blue will be the hue of the future.

Revival- and nostalgia-based design can benefit from these periods to capture a mood through color. For example, kids born after the '60s never saw the psychedelic movement, so when it was revived a generation later, the bright, bold colors were new to them, and they loved it. In the same vein, if you were young in the '70s, you didn't get tired of avocado green. So when it's available again, it's new to you. Or, if you loved harvest gold in the '70s, its use today— possibly with a slightly fresh spin— holds a kind of nostalgia for you, and can evoke some warm feelings, like hearing an old song that takes you back to that time and place where that song

was important to you. The psychedelic colors are used so successfully in the re-introduction of the VW bug. It's their tie to the '60s that Volkswagen is conveying by the use of the bright colors.

The psychology of color

Each color reaches us in a different way. Often we don't even recognize how we're affected. Understanding each color is critical to using it well and wisely in design.

Red. Red is the most studied and fascinating of all colors. It connotes excitement and danger, fire and bloodshed. Red can evoke a psychological fight-or-flight response: blood pressure and adrenaline rise, and hearts beat faster. We pay attention to red. It's a warning signal that is imprinted and reinforced generation after generation. It also has the most energy. Due to the physical stimulation associated with red, there is a sexual quality to the color. Because of this quality, red works well to underscore sexual allusions.

Blue. Blue is the opposite of red. We associate this color with serenity and tranquillity. Blue is seen in relation to

sky and water. We relate blue with dependability and constancy. This explains why certain types of blue are often used in company logos to evoke reliability.

Green. When people look at green, they see nature, which conveys a freshening and cleansing. Among the most-often-cited favorite colors—by consumers, as studied in color research—are the blue/greens because of the fresh and calm feelings associated with them. Therefore green works well to connote healthiness and freshness, for example.

Yellow. Yellow represents the sun in many cultures. Lighter yellows inspire a more cheerful, inviting feeling, while brighter yellows get more attention. Bright yellow is the most visible color. It's what our eye picks up first, so it's a good choice to grab attention, especially if highlighted with the opposite, cool colors—such as blue and green—that retreat in our field of vision.

Yellow and black are the most powerful color combination. Together these colors instinctively remind us of predatory animals and stinging insects. The attention-grabbing nature of the color combination remains with us today.

Cross-culturally, yellow evokes an upbeat, enthusiastic feeling. Therefore it works well when trying to convey happiness.

Orange. Orange is a combination of red and yellow, adopting qualities from both; it encompasses the excitement of red and the warmth and good cheer of yellow. Orange has a wide spectrum of hues, from brilliant neon to a softer, terra-cotta color. Because of the wide range of orange it's often the color that's the most misunderstood, and misused. Orange is a popular color for children, and therefore works well with toys and games. Because of its energy, orange is also associated with festivity and is a good choice when designing around celebrations or happy events.

Brown. Brown traditionally represents earth and dirt—both positive and negative. But recently the perception of brown has changed. It can now be associated with chocolate and coffee, gaining an air of deliciousness that it

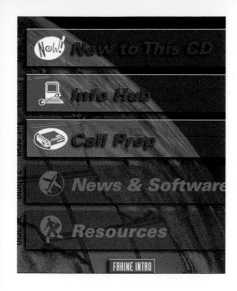

previously didn't have. Through the color associations with furs and dark woods, brown now has a more luxurious quality to it.

Outside the realm of the richness of coffee and chocolate, brown can evoke a sense of wholesomeness. How people feel about the color depends on the way brown is used. Often brown needs language associated with its design to properly connote the right mood.

Black. Black is a psychological color. At one time, black was considered funereal and associated with grief. But black now has an upscale aspect to it, evoking sophistication, power, and elegance. Black is a good choice when communicating a sense of elite or when targeting a design at a more urban audience.

Purple. Purple, a blend of red and blue, is the most complex of colors. Red makes purple hot and can bring out sensuousness in the hue, while the blue tones cool purple, making it more sedate and calming.

The heritage of purple and royalty dates back hundreds of years to European nobility. Originally purple was difficult to produce. Its dye was only available from a difficult-to-find snail whose shell had to be broken open to access the dye. Therefore, given its rarity, only royalty could afford the color. In some European cultures it was even declared that only royalty could wear purple.

Today purple is a good color choice when targeting creative types. Purple is so complex that it's effective when used with less traditional designs. It's often an underused color. As it has the element of red to it, it engenders excitement and causes us to stop and take notice. Purple is so unique that until recently there were few packages on the shelves dressed in this hue, other than Cadbury's chocolate in the UK, for which purple referenced a feeling of royalty.

Now that we've reviewed the colors and the reasons for web- or Browser-Safe Color, we'll explore some web sites that successfully celebrate color in their designs.

Nostalgic

To evoke the feeling of nostalgia, it's critical to capture the mood in image and in color—which, like other aspects of culture, has trends. Reflecting a certain era means bringing all the elements of design together, including typography, image, color, and copy. The two web sites in this chapter use color, along with other elements, to reinforce a message with nostalgia.

The Absinthe web site was created for the introduction of a new restaurant by that name in San Francisco. The primary palette on the home page consists of lime green, which reflects the milky, opalescent color of absinthe, and black, which plays to the darker side of this devilish beverage. To take advantage of the dark feel to the design, the art

director at 300 Feet Out in San Francisco, Janina Dietzel, decided to have some fun using amusing rollovers. Visitors can make the devil appear in the glass or make the lady blush.

The secondary palette, used for pages that include directions, menu, and press releases, is derived from posters and images of La Belle Epoque. The palette is muted and has little vibrancy. The design is infused with colors that evoke the dark corners in Parisian cafés at the opening of the twentieth century, where artists, writers, and musicians lingered over their absinthe and discussed the issues of the day. "It really is an updated feeling for the romantic notion of the time that we were trying to capture," says Dietzel.

Absinthe

MENU

BREAKFAST

BRUNCH

LUNCH

BAR

DINNER

OYSTER BAR

CHEESE

When capturing the mood of a fast-rising band in San Francisco, designer Mark Wyman knew exactly what he wanted. "The band Casino Royale celebrates the vibrancy and, in some ways, the innocence of the 1960s. I needed to capture this freshness in the design." Wyman took the psychedelic colors of that decade as the base of his palette. "I used the excitement of Carnaby Street as my background." His choice of colors reflects the fun and youthfulness of the time. The web site, www.casinoroyalemusic.com, promotes the band and its growth. By including the nostalgic colors that contribute to the band's shows, Wyman communicates their spirit and energy through effective web design.

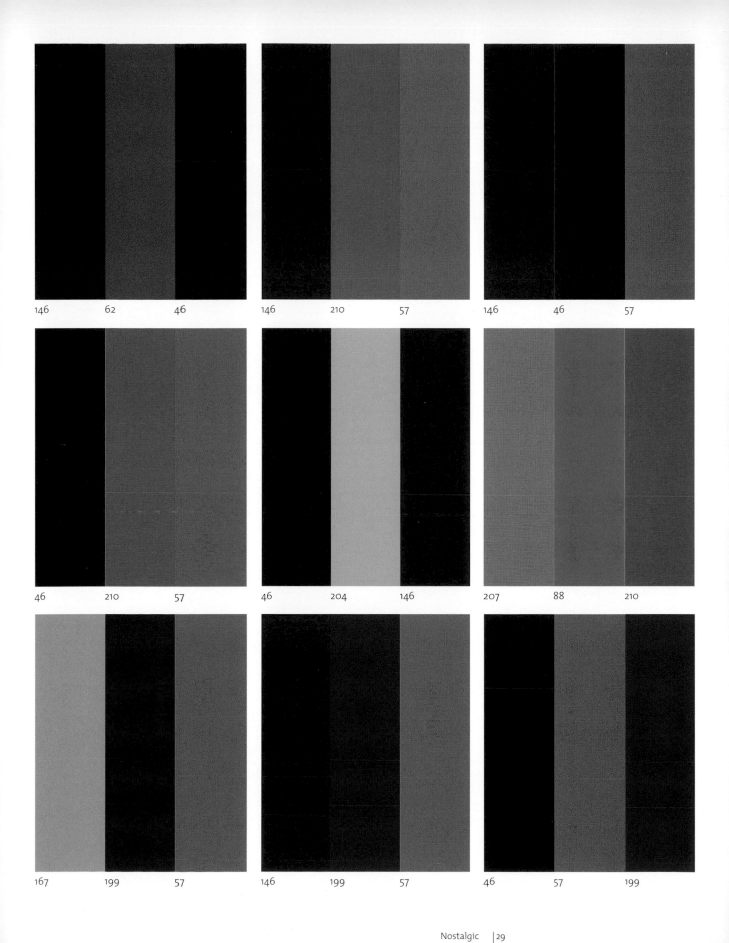

| 146 | 62 | 46 | | 146 | 210 | 57 | | 146 | 46 | 57 |

| 46 | 210 | 57 | | 46 | 204 | 146 | | 207 | 88 | 210 |

| 167 | 199 | 57 | | 146 | 199 | 57 | | 46 | 57 | 199 |

| 118 | 46 | 146 | | 146 | 46 | 210 | | 199 | 46 | 146 |

| 46 | 137 | 57 | | 46 | 137 | 62 | | 137 | 207 | 62 |

| 137 | 62 | 199 | | 118 | 88 | 57 | | 118 | 204 | 57 |

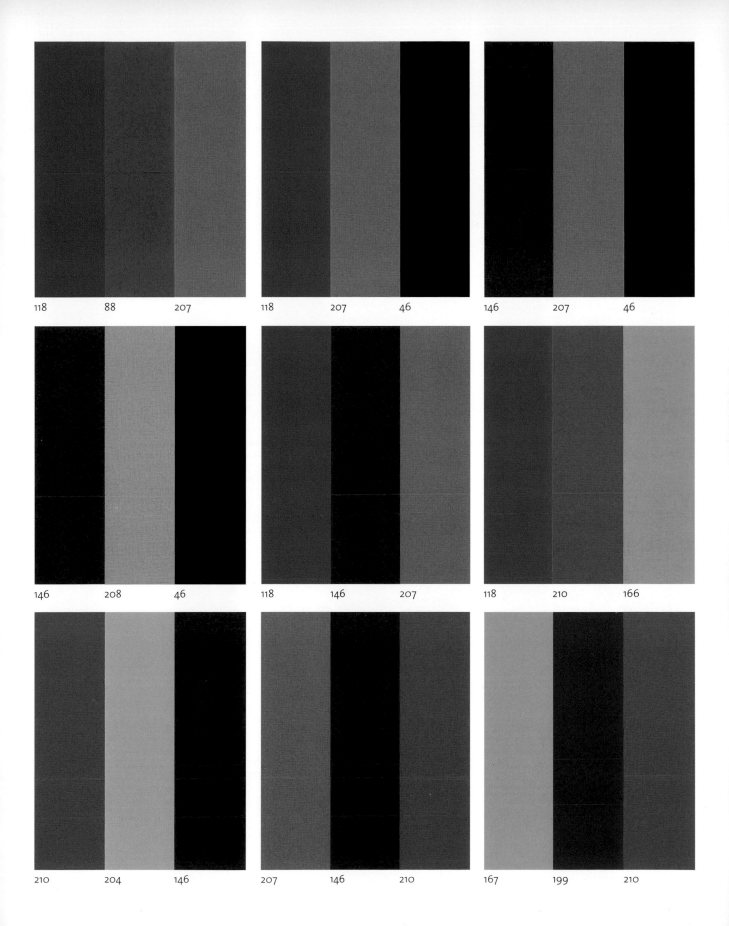

118	88	207
118	207	46
146	207	46

146	208	46
118	146	207
118	210	166

210	204	146
207	146	210
167	199	210

118	167	207
46	208	118
46	118	204

199	204	210
199	207	146
118	146	199

118	199	57
199	88	207
199	88	158

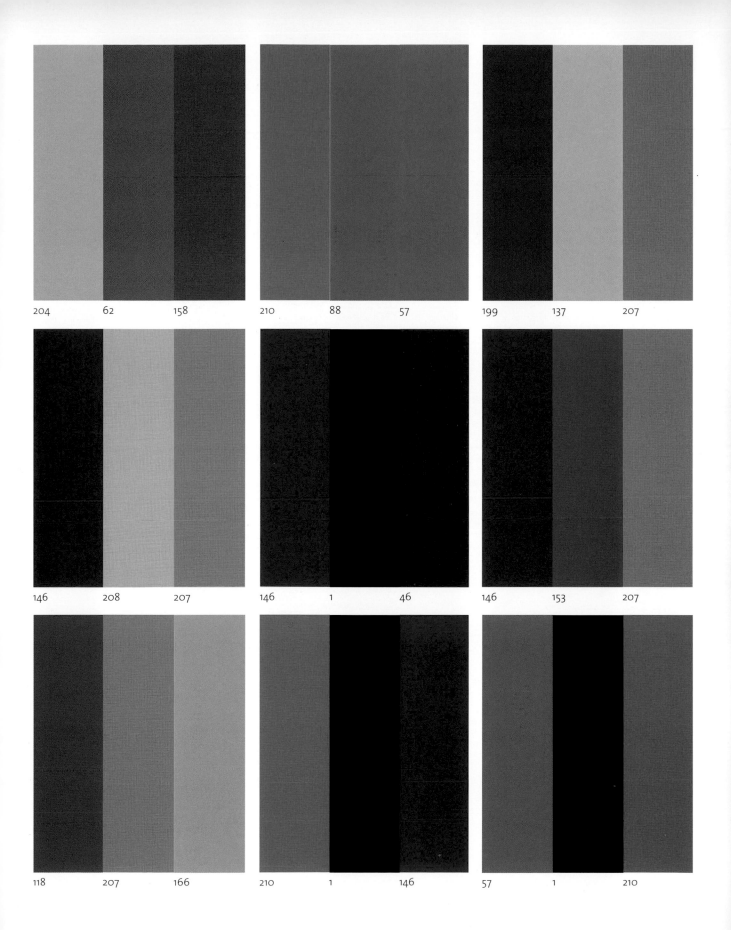

204   62   158   210   88   57   199   137   207

146   208   207   146   1   46   146   153   207

118   207   166   210   1   146   57   1   210

Multicultural

To capture a multicultural feel, colors are critical. West African Highlife, a band-specific web site, is an excellent example of the power of color in design. Bay Area web site designer Joshua Jacobson wanted to communicate the band's African roots through the design. "The colors of the site capture the feeling of African culture but also appeal to people not from Africa," he says. The earthy green and brown are distinctly noncommercial. The yellow and orange background evokes the sunlight of Africa. "I used the highlight colors as the principal hues on later pages to give a sense of lifting the curtain to let people in," Jacobson says. One of the fonts used on the inside pages was created by an African typographer, adding to the African origins of the site. By blending traditionally African colors with appropriate design, Jacobson created a site that expresses the roots of the band while remaining accessible for newcomers.

Atlas magazine was established in 1994 as a forum for photography, multimedia, and web-based design. This issue of the online magazine was inspired by rural Chinese architecture. Amy Franceschini of Futurefarmers, a San Francisco design firm, chose colors that evoke the Chinese countryside. "The colors relate to the primary story," she says. The reds and pinks continue the colors of Chinese costume, yet the tones

① editorial

② photography

③ cyberbilly

④ paradise online

are muted, giving an ethereal feel to the site. By using colors that are inspired by feelings of rural China, Franceschini has created a design that piques the visitor's curiosity, drawing the reader in to the content inside.

The Kotoja site, dedicated to a Bay Area band, was created in 1998. The band's lead singer is Nigerian and other members are from around the world, a diversity reflected in the African-based world music they play. The design colors combine world influences with African roots. Designs that build on African colors often use bright yellows, to evoke the ever-present African sun, and rich browns to bring the color of the land into the design. "The tones are earthy, accented by highly saturated colors," says designer Jacobson. His bright use of orangey tones with deep blue accents provide vivid contrasts for this site, and offer a warm and friendly feel. The drawings of the band members extend the feeling of fun accessibility, while the non-symmetrical angles of the boxes on the home page add a dynamic quality. By mixing deep colors with rich, bright hues, Jacobson created a site that is accessible to a broad audience, yet captures the world feeling of the band. The Kotoja site is an excellent example of a color palette that is inspired by a location, then enhanced with accent colors to expand the reach of the site.

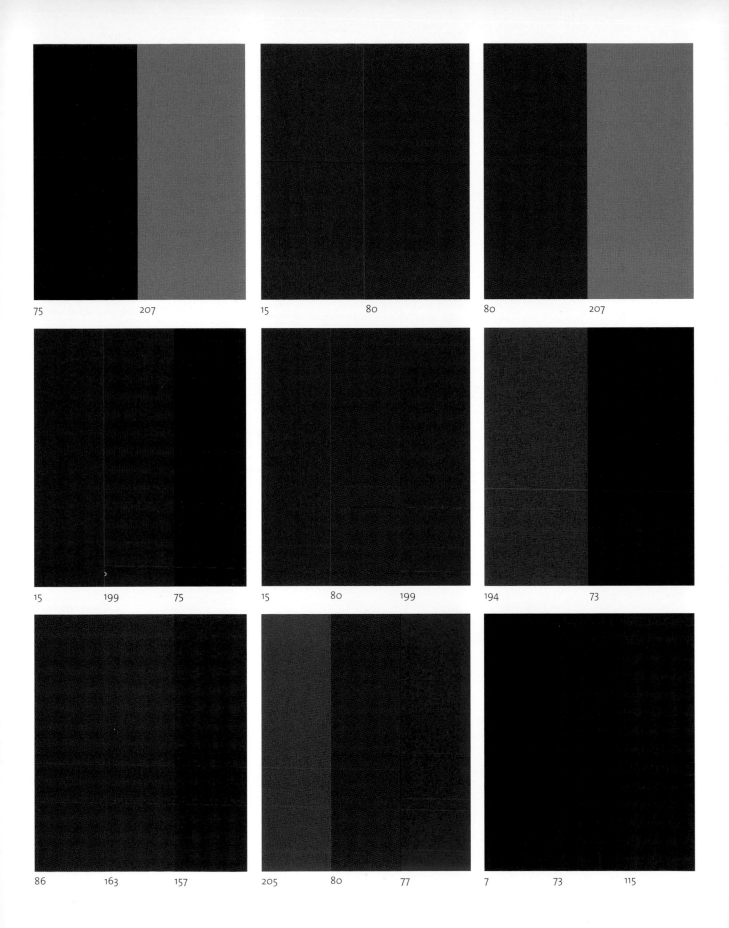

207

15 80

80 207

15 199 75

15 80 199

194 73

86 163 157

205 80 77

7 73 115

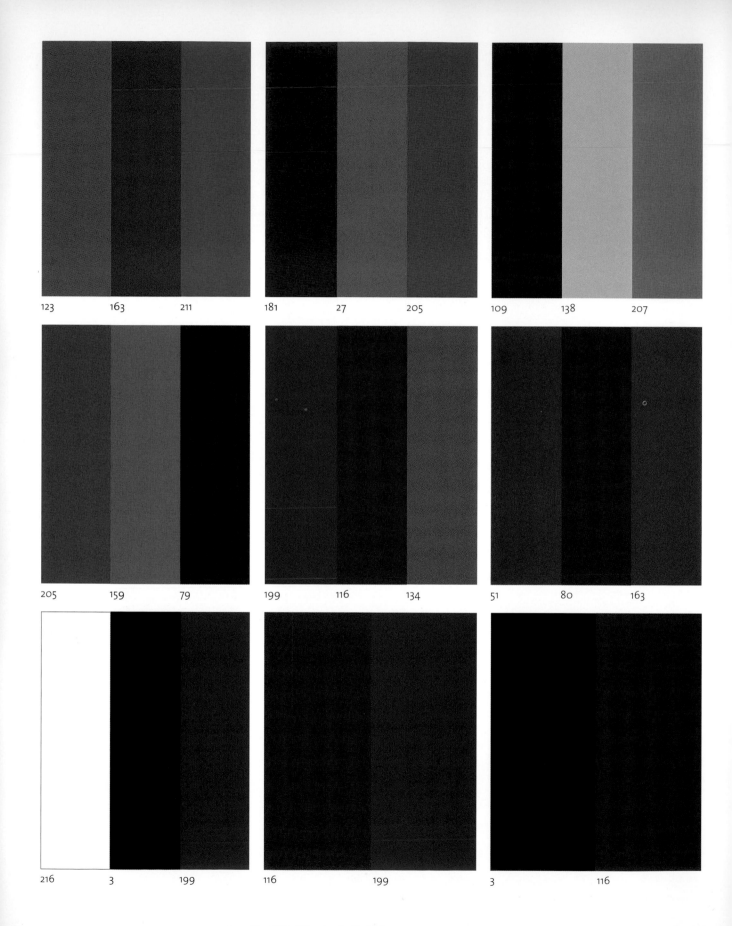

123   163   211   181   27   205   109   138   207

205   159   79   199   116   134   51   80   163

216   3   199   116   199   3   116

117   200

9   199

6   199

109   39   193

3   165

73   200

116   87

199   79

201   8   47

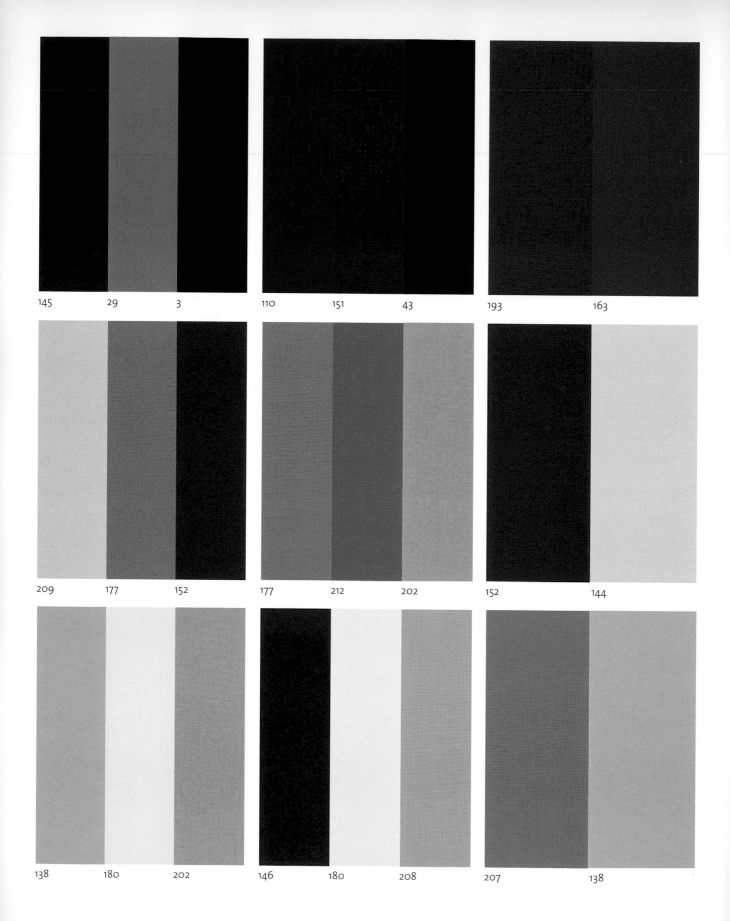

145   29   3   110   151   43   193   163

209   177   152   177   212   202   152   144

138   180   202   146   180   208   207   138

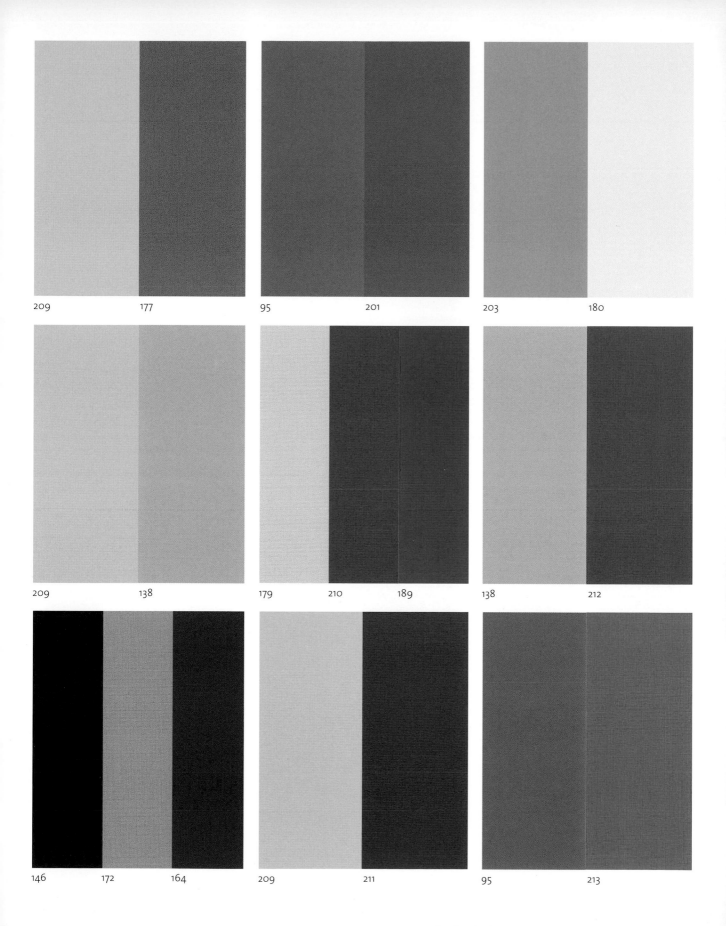

209   177   95   201   203   180

209   138   179   210   189   138   212

146   172   164   209   211   95   213

Fresh

Savvio is a site for time-constrained, value-driven consumers who want to quickly research and purchase travel-related products and services online. The site needs to capture the visitor's attention and draw them in quickly. The creative team at 300 Feet Out in San Francisco knew that color would be a large part of the design's effectiveness. "The orange and gray were chosen as corporate colors for Savvio," says Anna Bervander, designer. For the home page, yellow was selected to enliven the design and to get visitors excited about Savvio's patented pricing model. The yellow extends into the search section, and turquoise indicates the transaction pages. The freshness of the colors adds to the excitement that consumers feel when using this money-saving web site.

Neiman Marcus is an upscale store targeted to upper-income women. In designing the site, it was critical that the creative team at Rare Medium in San Francisco capture the elegance of the store while maintaining freshness. The site was designed to be updated seasonally, allowing for ongoing product promotions. "We created a site that allows for regular color changes to indicate new product introductions," says Tim Barber, creative director. The company can update the colors without changing the site. The spring 1999 colors were fresh greens. The two tones—a bright green with a deeper green accent—capture the feeling of the season while working within the elegant design.

Neiman Marcus

APRIL 1999

THE BOOK
STORE INFO
SERVICES
ようこそ

As seen in W magazine...

BEAUTY
BOOK

NM
NOTE
BOOKS

ON THE COVER

Born in California, cover artist Colleen Silva spent her
early childhood in Pakistan. She returned to the United
States, attended Berkeley, and then moved to Paris to
work with an esteemed hat designer. After eight years
as an account executive at a French advertising agency,
she moved to Idaho where, in addition to tutoring the

The seasonal tone updates alert regular visitors that new items are available. Wanting to maintain a fresh feel throughout the year, the design team chose bright color palettes that create excitement about the new products highlighted on the page. In another season, the colors were rich orange and brown. By creatively selecting colors in the same family, with deeply saturated tones and strong accent choices, Rare Medium created a sense of ongoing newness critical for a successful e-commerce site.

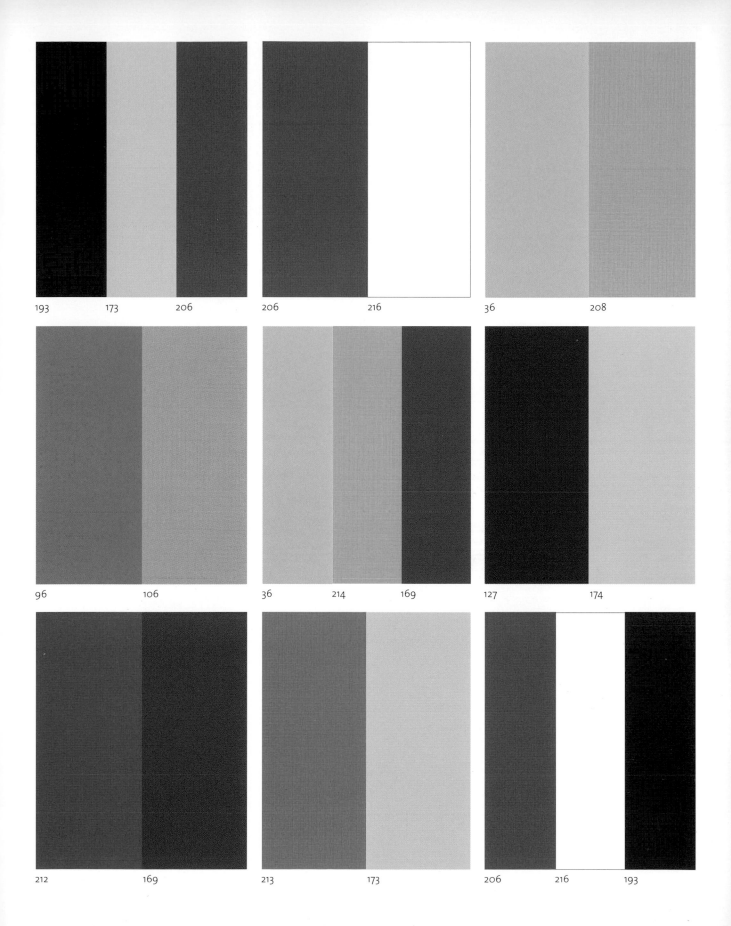

193   173   206   206   216   36   208

96   106   36   214   169   127   174

212   169   213   173   206   216   193

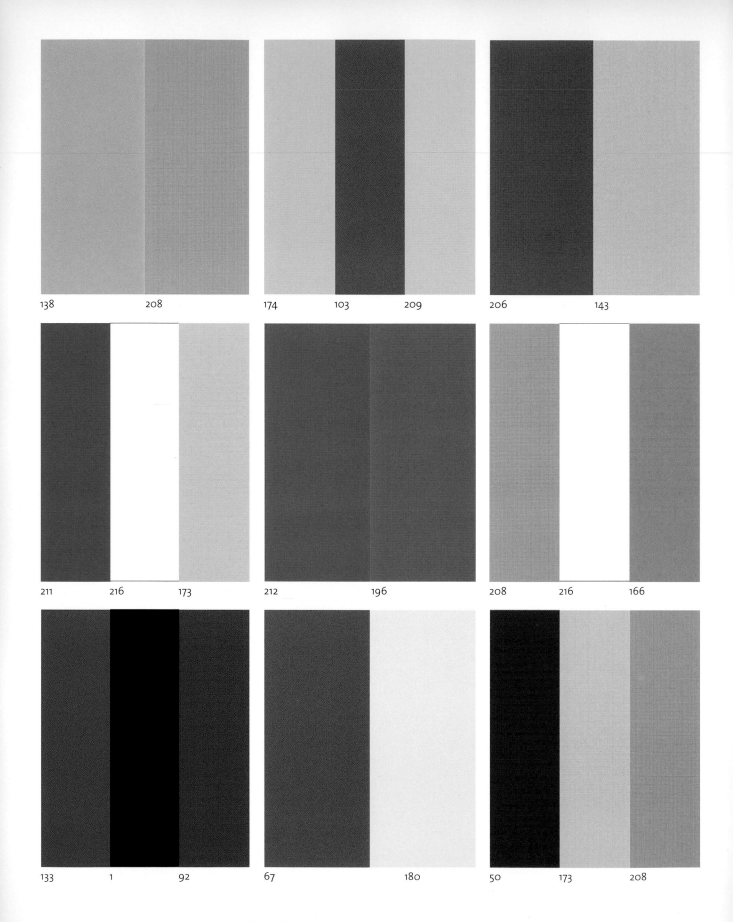

138   208   174   103   209   206   143

211   216   173   212   196   208   216   166

133   1   92   67   180   50   173   208

67   1   208   178   1   138   169   208

175   144   91   131   208   130   127

31   174   121   169   169   216   202

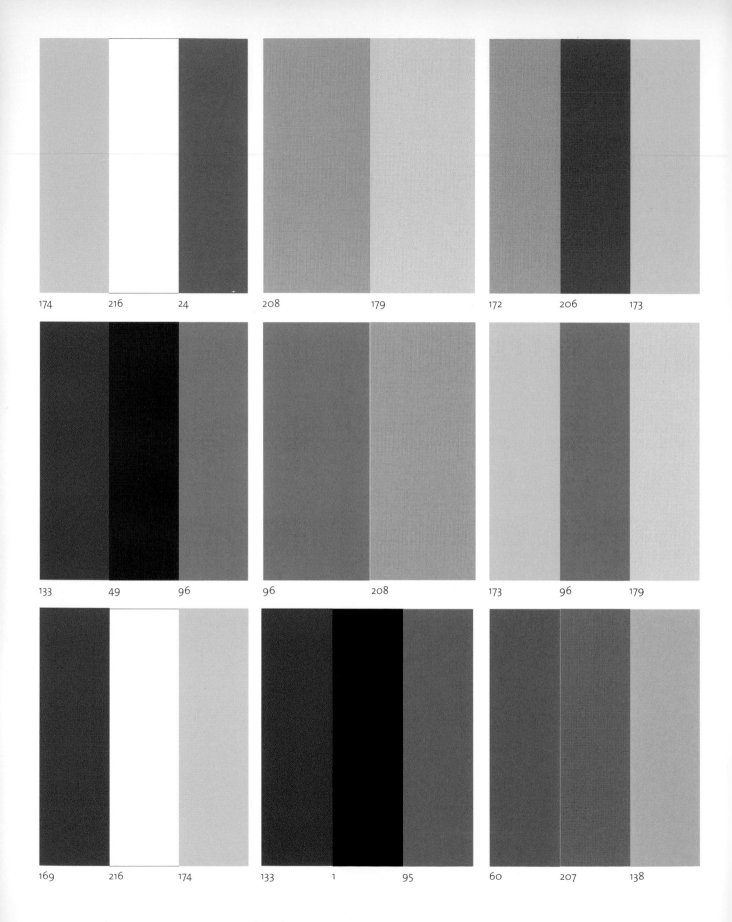

174   216   24

208   179

172   206   173

133   49   96

96   208

173   96   179

169   216   174

133   1   95

60   207   138

211 166 132   108 215   19 216 169

164 177   31 180 207   138 87 212

208 172 199   212 138   180 96

Earthy

With the Invivo site, Kim Webb at Webb Design in San Francisco chose colors for their muted, earthy qualities. The site is aimed at the medical profession and offers healthcare-related software solutions via the Palm hand-held device. Given the tones of the corporate logo, Webb chose tones that are subdued and calming without being traditionally corporate. "We chose colors that are easy to look at and that evoke simplicity, which reflects the product," says Webb. "And the color palette must work on the Web and on the Palm's smaller screen." The subdued hues are inspired by sky and sea colors. The tones are rarely combined, but when they do come together, their effect is so immediate that they offer a familiar yet fresh take on a color palette and convey an assurance and accessibility critical to the product's branding.

The Terrascope home page was designed to give a look of finesse to the company's web site. "We played with colors," says Bill Dunlap at Terrascope in San Francisco, a web site design firm. "We looked at colors that were not necessarily web safe. We wanted a professional, serious site that was cool, clean, and polished, yet had a playful side." The name *Terrascope* is built on the Latin word for earth, so the designers first reviewed earthy colors. "Then we added a bright blue for the sky, so looking at our site would remind one of viewing a landscape," says Steve Bishop of Terrascope. The result is a distinctive and memorable combination.

On the secondary pages of the Terrascope site, the creative team at the firm extended the design by prominently using a rich range of blues. The firm's choice of tones evokes the expanse of the sky, which communicates a sense of security. The breadth of the blues, from deep tones to light morning sky blues, bring a relaxed, assuring and spacious feel to the site, communicating an openness and broadness of view that reflects the culture of the design firm. By combining intense blues with select highlight colors—pinks, beiges and browns, all colors that evoke the stability of the earth—Terrascope created a vivid yet calming design that captures the creativity and expansiveness of their work. This imagery is used across its secondary pages, with each page expanding on a different color. From the fluid arcs and the repeating boxes to the horizon-enforcing lines, Terrascope has taken its name and spirit, and developed an effective, evocative look and feel. With layers of reinforcing imagery and branding, they have created a site that delivers a simplicity and elegance while communicating the expansiveness that is Terrascope.

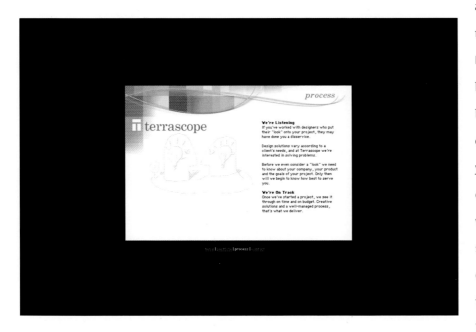

94   172   130

172   79

94   85

121   172   94

121   87   109

85   109

79   91   88

21   170

50   122   94

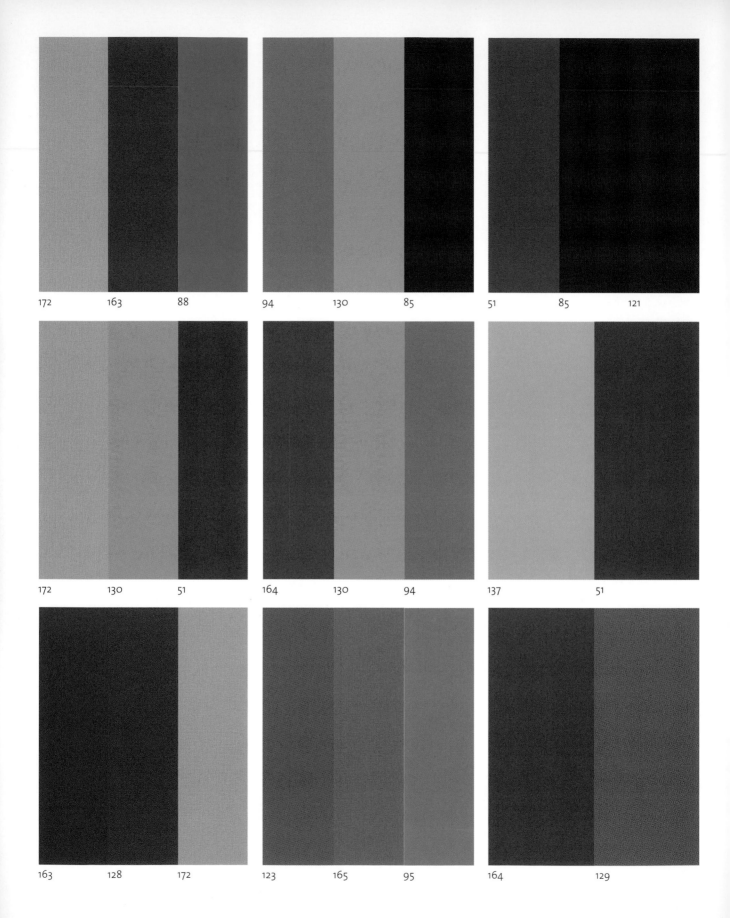

172   163   88

94   130   85

51   85   121

172   130   51

164   130   94

137   51

163   128   172

123   165   95

164   129

Color Harmony for the Web

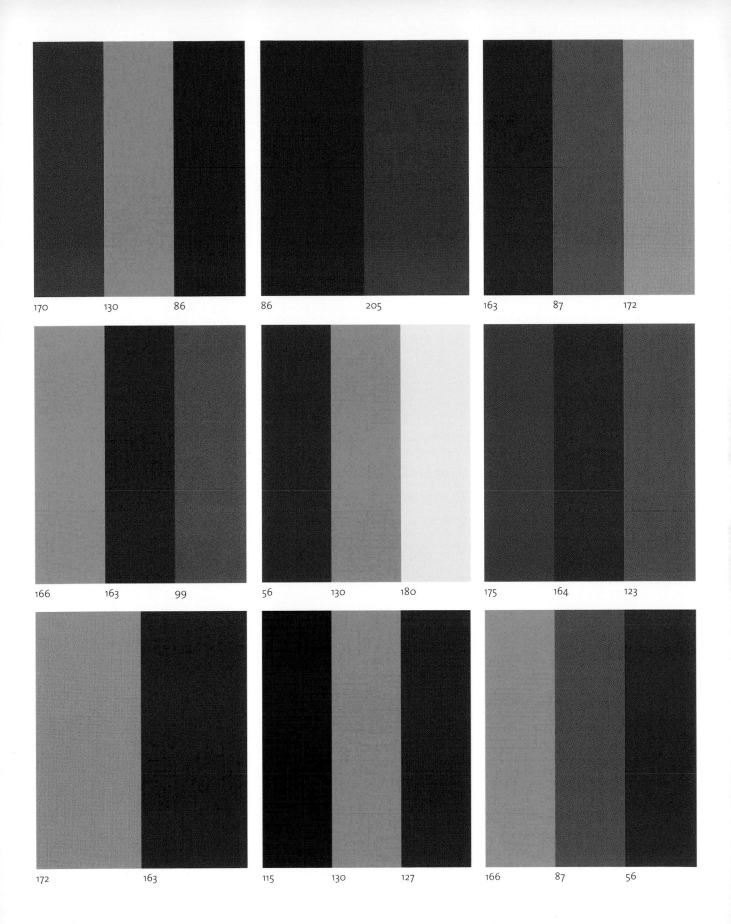

170   130   86   86   205   163   87   172

166   163   99   56   130   180   175   164   123

172   163   115   130   127   166   87   56

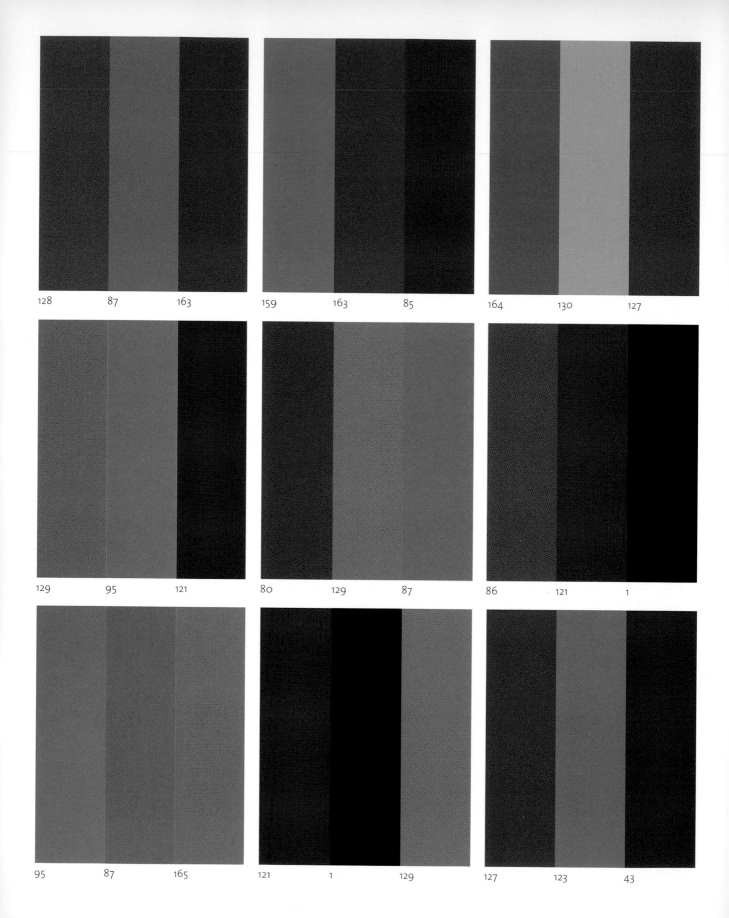

128   87   163

159   163   85

164   130   127

129   95   121

80   129   87

86   121   1

95   87   165

121   1   129

127   123   43

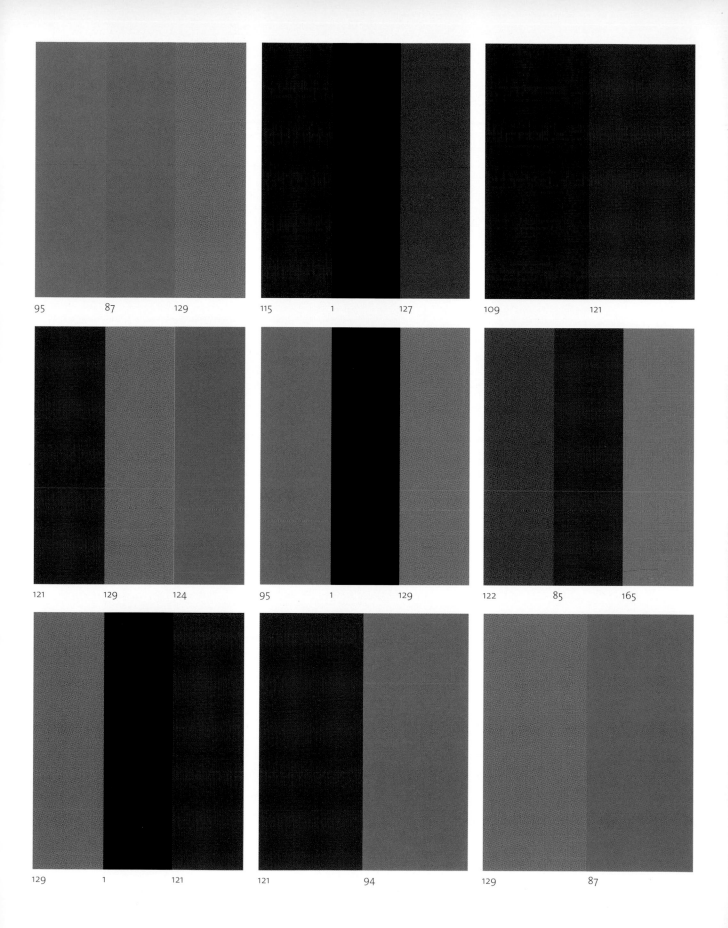

95   87   129   115   1   127   109   121

121   129   124   95   1   129   122   85   165

129   1   121   121   94   129   87

Lively

Color Paramount is a color separator and digital prepress house for advertising agencies; therefore, their site had to appeal to refined design taste. The choice of tones began with the lively corporate colors of Color Paramount—bright yellow with orange and green highlights. "The web site had to demonstrate the high level of design sensibility and attention to detail that is Color Paramount's reputation," says Lane Good of Fast Lane Studios. Against the black background, the images rotating on the home page bounce off the screen, highlighting Color Paramount's work.

Another range of lively colors is seen in the designs for NEC's Lumina, a subsection of the company's global site that showcases ongoing research and development efforts in hardware technology. Feature stories highlight NEC scientists and their projects. To create the design for these pages, Terry Green, of twenty2product in San Francisco, began with colors from the world map palette. "We had the sonogram of the world," says Green. "Then we elevated the importance of the color." Green applied the vivid tones that come from the globe and the array of color indicating weather throughout the design. The bright reds, yellows, and blues on the introductory page bring to it a lively, exciting feel, enticing viewers to click through to the following pages to read about NEC's world of discovery.

PUBLISHER'S NOTE

LUMINA

NEC

The brightness of the design is carried through the inside pages. The colors of the world weather map both challenge and enhance the familiar and unique designs of the site. Repeating circles suggestive of CD-ROMs contrast with the rectangular shapes that form a photo-like frame. Beginning with a world image on the left, then breaking the globe into weather-based areas, and imposing on that vacation-based images, Green has given us a vivid, design that celebrates the feelings that color evokes. Using the spectrum, the viewer feels the effect of color, from coolness of blues and the freshness of greens to the heat of reds. This inventive use of imagery and tone allows the visual choices to transport the viewer to locations that reinforce the feeling of the colors. The heat of the reds and oranges take the viewer to the warmth of the beach, while colder tones in the blues impart a sense of coolness from polar regions. With the clever use of color as a metaphor for travel and global experience, Green has communicated the worldwide reach of NEC and its ideas, while bringing the company out of traditional corporate imagery, to the world of freedom suggested in the design.

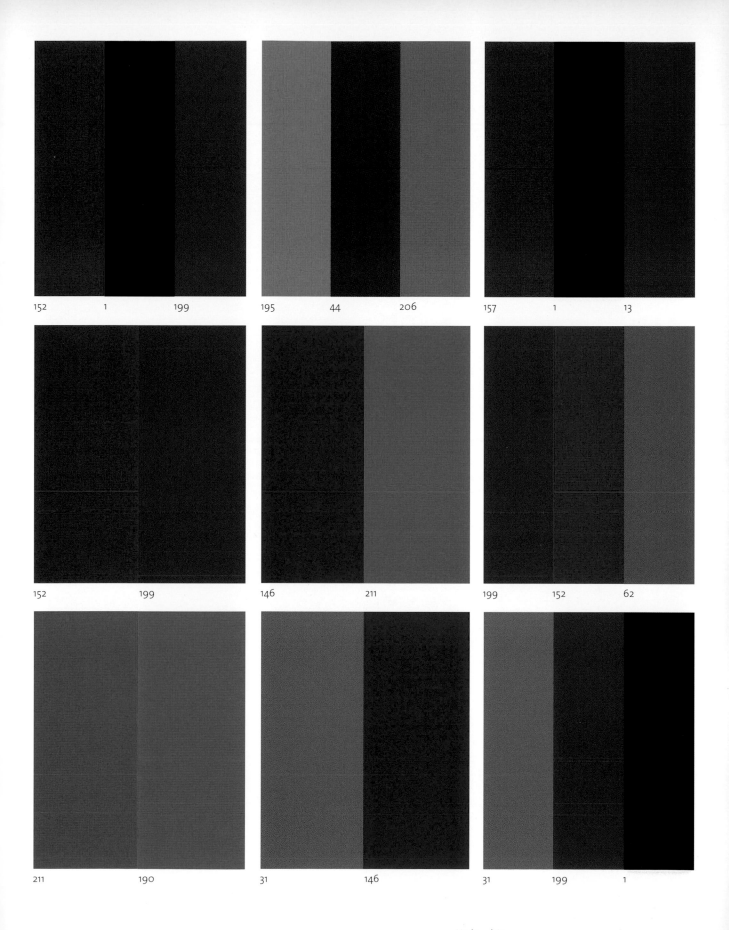

152   1   199

195   44   206

157   1   13

152   199

146   211

199   152   62

211   190

31   146

31   199   1

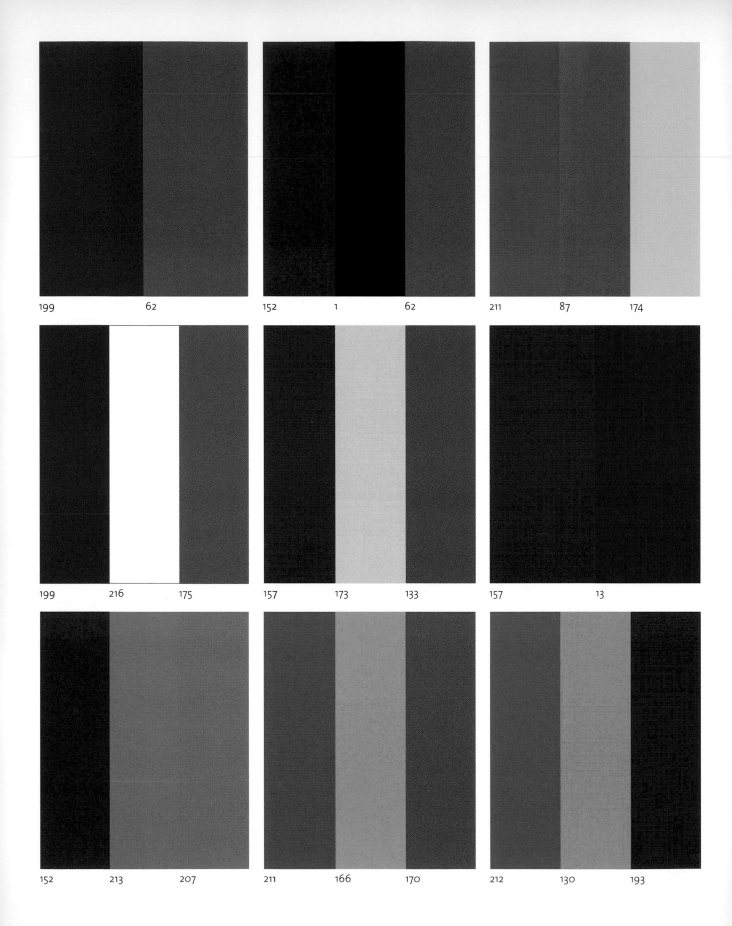

199   62

152   1   62

211   87   174

199   216   175

157   173   133

157   13

152   213   207

211   166   170

212   130   193

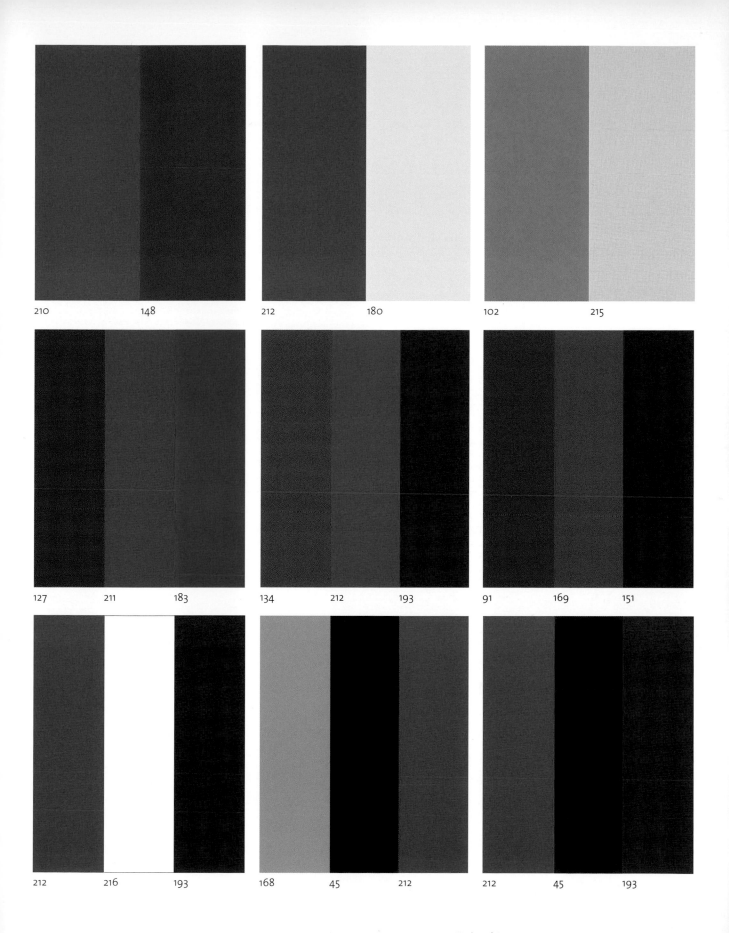

210   148   212   180   102   215

127   211   183   134   212   193   91   169   151

212   216   193   168   45   212   212   45   193

3   212   134   212   134   3   193

3   193   168   181   211   67   193   173   169

20   211   211   102   208   166   134

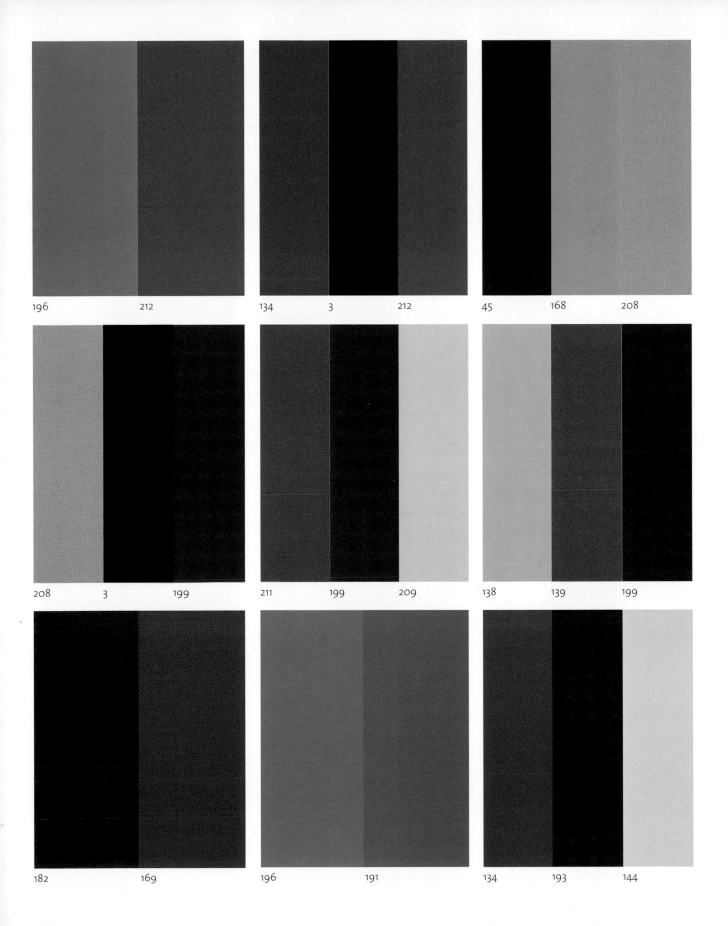

196   212

134   3   212

45   168   208

208   3   199

211   199   209

138   139   199

182   169

196   191

134   193   144

Romantic

To express romance, tones need to be rich in mood and the design needs to be soft and evocative. The redesigned Britney Spears web site achieves this, perfectly capturing the romance surrounding the teen singing sensation. "Her site needed to reflect her as a celebrity and as a young woman," says Karen Shields, creative director at DNA Visual Business Solutions in Chicago. "Her previous site was younger and, her management felt, no longer reflected her or her audience."

Signature Networks, which oversees merchandising and licensing for Britney, approached DNA in Chicago to give her site an updated look, making it more lively and accessible. "We chose the jewel tones for a more young adult feel," says Jessica Schnepf, visual designer at DNA. By keeping the colors in the deep family of romantic tones, such as jade greens, ruby reds, and sapphire blues, the designers captured the bright, fun-loving nature of the pop star and her music while giving her images a rich feel. They added beautiful photos that download quickly and work perfectly with the color tones. "Now the site is more sophisticated," says Shields. "It's more for the fans."

britney spears

GALLERY

PHOTOS | video clips | backstage

FAN CLUB

STORE

photos

Wonder what Britney's up to? Check out the pix of photo sessions, concerts, or just hang loose and get to know the real Britney.

video clips

Would you like to spend a day with Britney? Go on a road trip with Britney! See video clips you won't see anywhere else!

backstage

Get an exclusive backstage pass into Britney's world. Catch her hanging out with her dancers, friends, and family.

The textured backgrounds complement the rich, romantic colors. Each section has color tones that identify the area of the site. The home page and Cool Stuff page builds on extraordinarily rich sapphire blues with a textured background that enhance each image. Your Stuff celebrates jade greens to complement the image of Britney in the outdoors. The FAQ page uses amethyst tones to create a beautiful frame for the exquisite image. The Gallery page and Tour Info page make brilliant use of pinks and ruby reds while the News page is drenched in shades of lively orange. By using vivid hues to evoke the mood of her music, the designers captured the image of the artist. The tones are upbeat and romantic, like the singer and her songs. "We wanted colors that make you happy when you look at them. With the beautiful photos of Britney, I know we've developed a site that her fans enjoy, and that you'd come to expect from Britney — stylish, more sophisticated, yet still fun and accessible. And I know that the choice of color had a lot to do with this successful web site," says Shields.

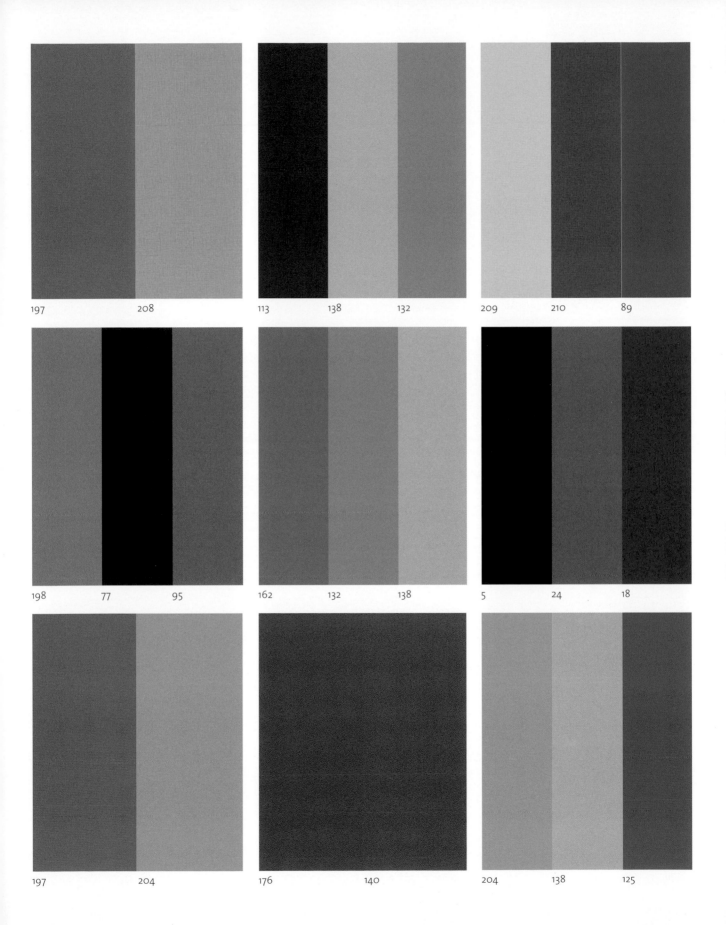

197   208

113   138   132

209   210   89

198   77   95

162   132   138

5   24   18

197   204

176   140

204   138   125

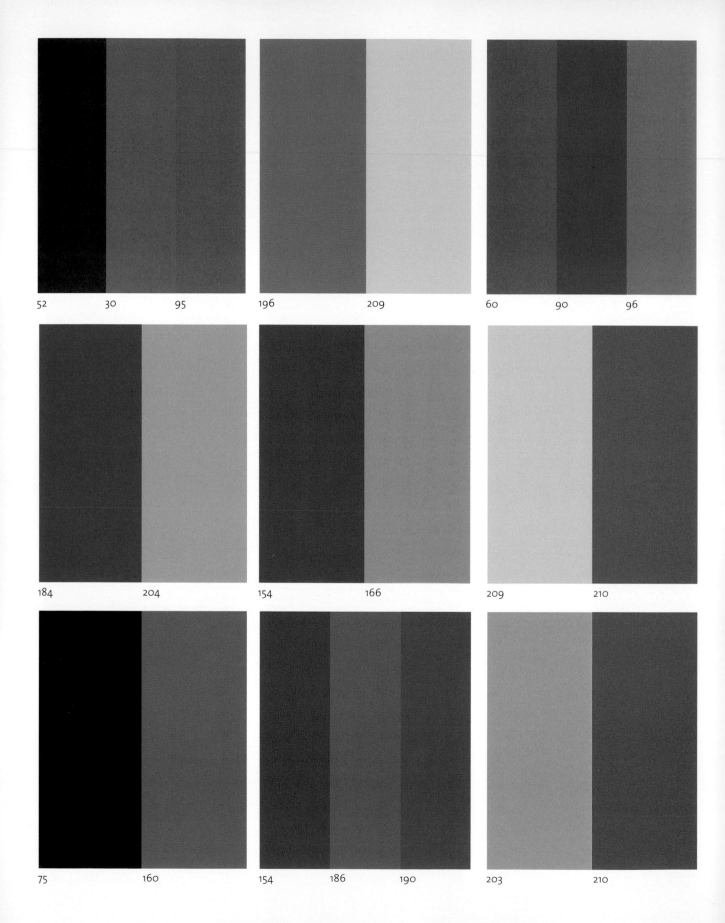

52   30   95   196   209   60   90   96

184   204   154   166   209   210

75   160   154   186   190   203   210

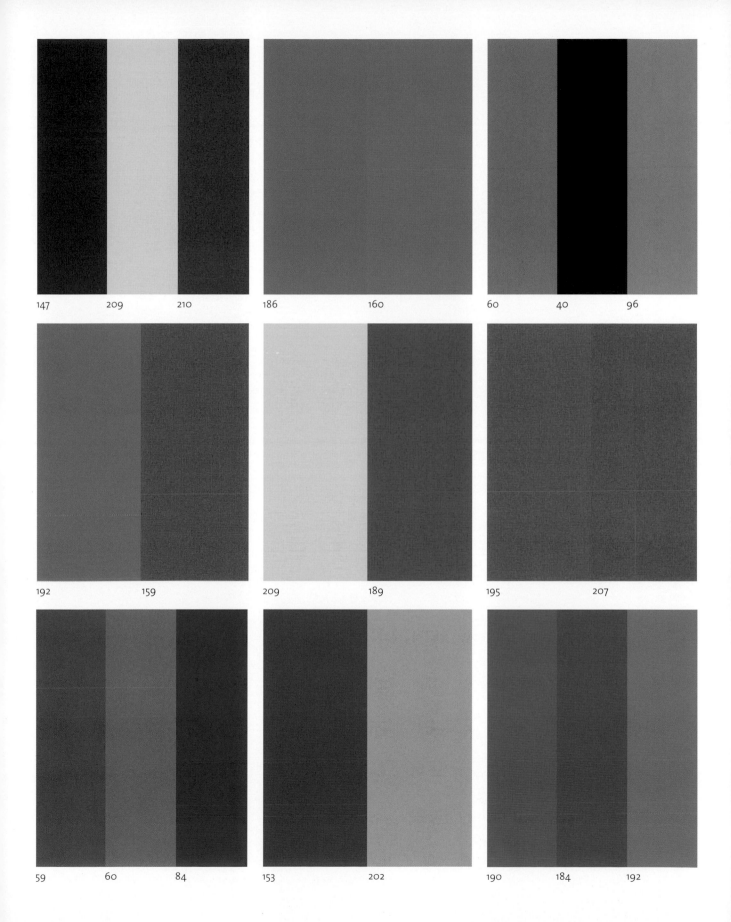

147   209   210   186   160   60   40   96

192   159   209   189   195   207

59   60   84   153   202   190   184   192

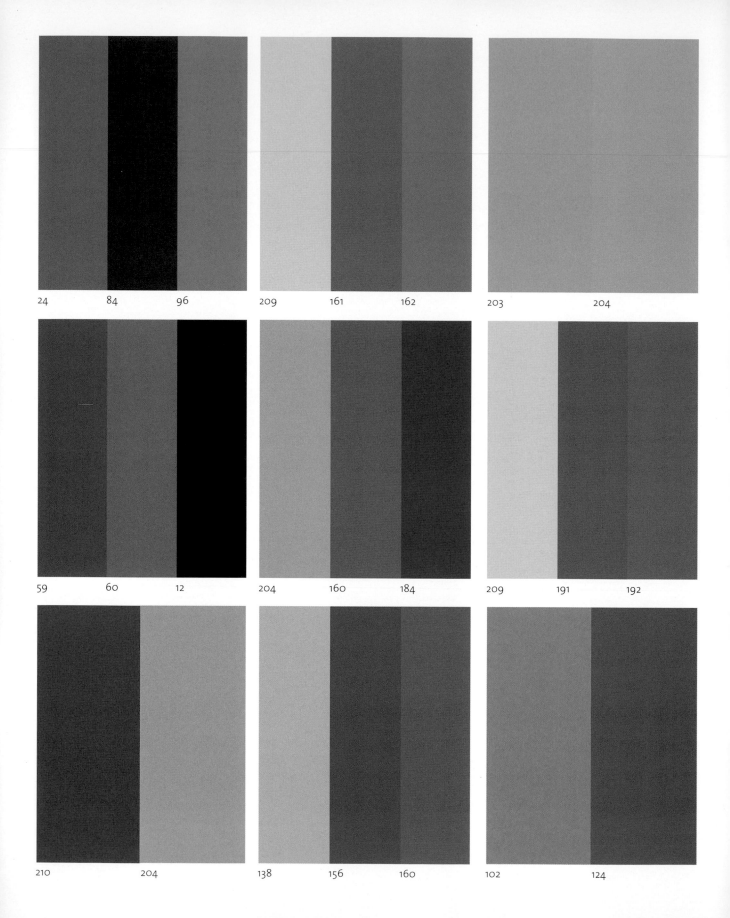

24   84   96

209   161   162

203   204

59   60   12

204   160   184

209   191   192

210   204

138   156   160

102   124

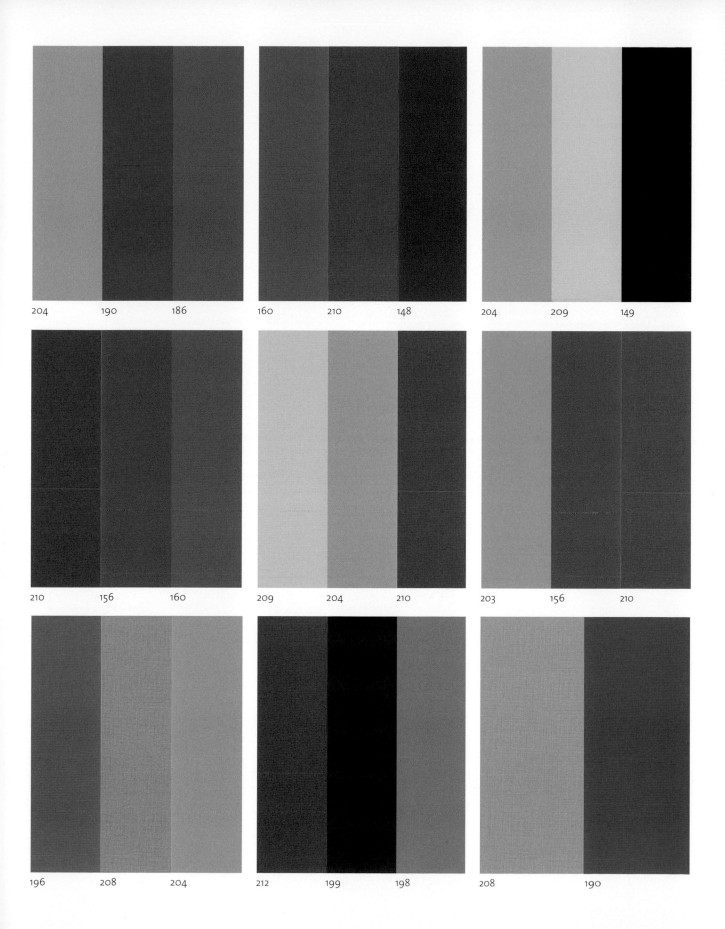

204 190 186

160 210 148

204 209 149

210 156 160

209 204 210

203 156 210

196 208 204

212 199 198

208 190

Energetic

Venus Sports is a retail web site that also provides sports information and resources for the growing community of active women. VenusSports.com acts as a partner for female athletes by offering a one-stop place for personalized training, schedules, articles, and equipment. To capture the energy that drives the company and its customers, the design team at 300 Feet Out in San Francisco needed to choose just the right colors to match their unique designs. It was critical that the design be dynamic without being too aggressive. The lively, active, sophisticated colors and graphics engage visitors and draw them into the site.

"We chose lime green and a dark blue as the corporate colors for Venus Sports," says Anna Bervander, designer at 300 Feet Out. In creating an atmosphere for the e-commerce site, specific background colors were chosen to indicate the various sports categories, while the top and the side navigation remain in the corporate colors. "Our challenge was to design an overall Venus Sports atmosphere where the e-commerce section is embedded in the design and maintains equal importance in the content area," says Bervander. Throughout the site, the energy and excitement of the colors are prominent.

VENUS V SPORTS
.com

news · articles · community · my account · cart

Search our site

[ ] **GO**

Sport
Select...Sport ▼

Product
Select...Product ▼

Brand
Select...Brand ▼

Personalized Shopper
RECOMMENGINE

>>> Cycling

Page 1 2 3

Tops
Bottoms
Footwear
Accessories
Equipment
Nutrition

Home>Scores and News: Womens NCAA Basketball

Athletic Tops

Giordano
Short Sleeve Jersey
$69.00

Terry
Bike Seat
$119.95

Rudy Project
Sunglasses
$78.95

Terry
Bike Seat
$119.95

Giordano
Short Sleeve Jersey
$69.00

Terry
Bike Seat
$119.95

Rudy Project
Sunglasses
$78.95

Terry
Bike Seat
$119.95

Page 1 2 3

About Us   Privacy & Security   Customer Service   Terms & Conditions
© 2000 VenusSports.com All Rights Reserved

The colors of the Xpedior site bring bold energy to the screen. The company is a consulting firm that provides innovative and comprehensive e-business solutions to Global 2000 companies and emerging Internet businesses. From the black and green of the logo to the roll-over colors, the site evokes movement. "We were looking for a fresher, non-corporate look," says Chip Taylor at Xpedior. "The biggest challenge for this site was to establish the brand, and our choice and use of color were a large part of this. We had to create a color palette that would work well on the screen and translate to print and collateral material." By selecting bright, bold, energetic colors that complement the Xpedior logo, the web site communicates the approachable, accessible nature of the company. The yellow of the logo, set off by the background black, makes a bold statement. The vitality in the color palette is continued on the secondary pages. While the secondary pages are more content-intensive, the header and sidebar of each page richly complement the logo in tones that range from cooler blues and purples to warmer yellows and oranges. The use of tone in the colors used adds a sense of depth and movement, a feeling that is continued with the subtle horizontal lines in the header of the pages. From logo color to complementary secondary palette and design, the site evokes an energy that captures the feeling of Xpedior and helps position it and its branding.

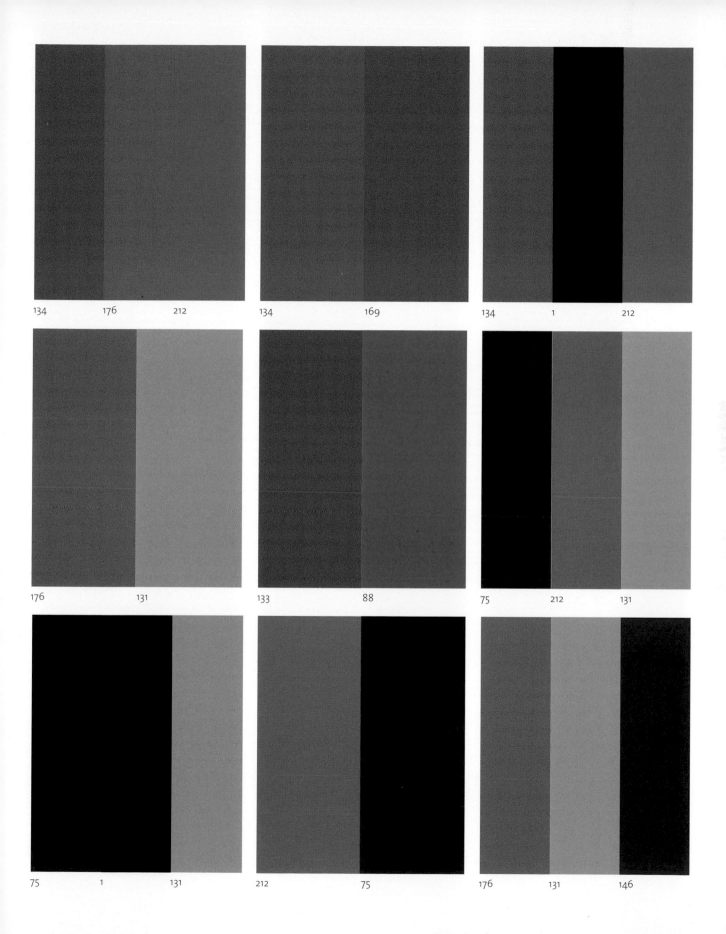

134   176   212

134   169

134   1   212

176   131

133   88

75   212   131

75   1   131

212   75

176   131   146

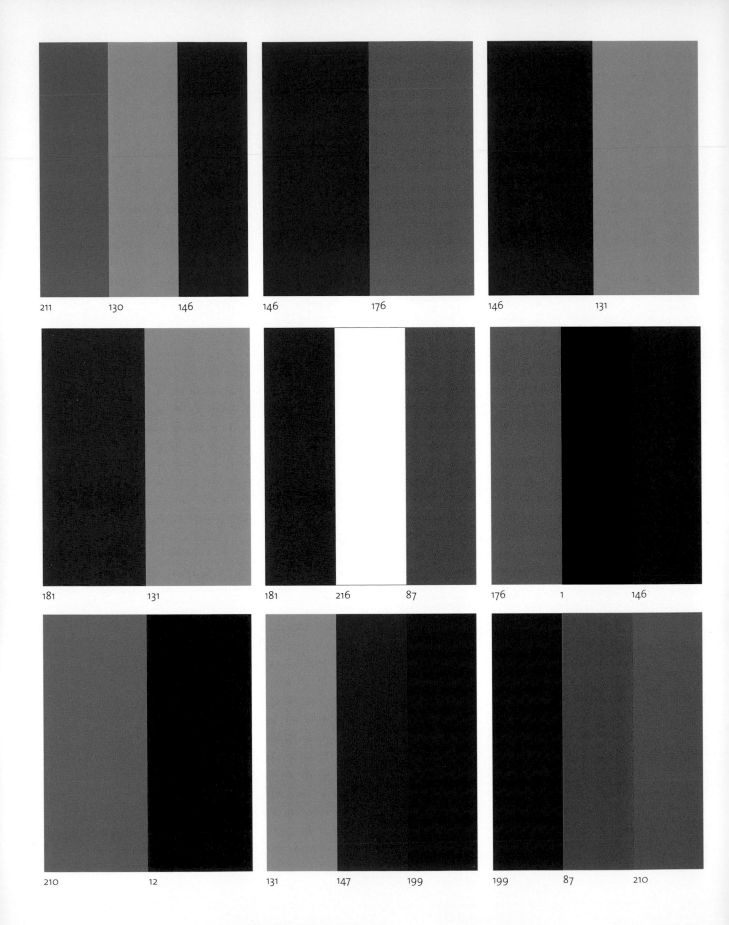

211   130   146   146   176   146   131

181   131   181   216   87   176   1   146

210   12   131   147   199   199   87   210

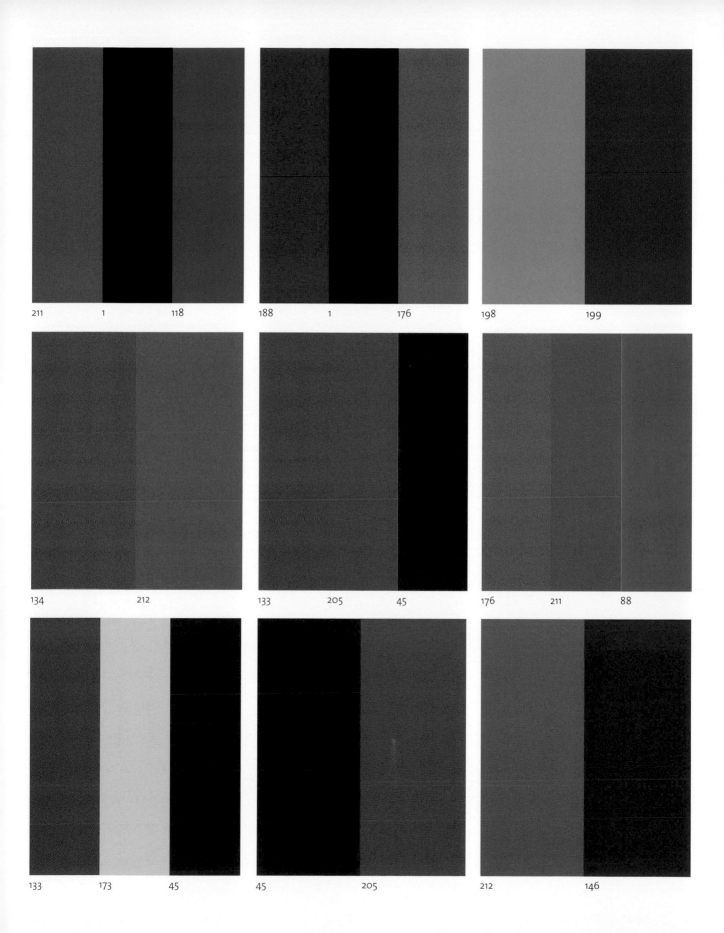

211   1   118   188   1   176   198   199

134   212   133   205   45   176   211   88

133   173   45   45   205   212   146

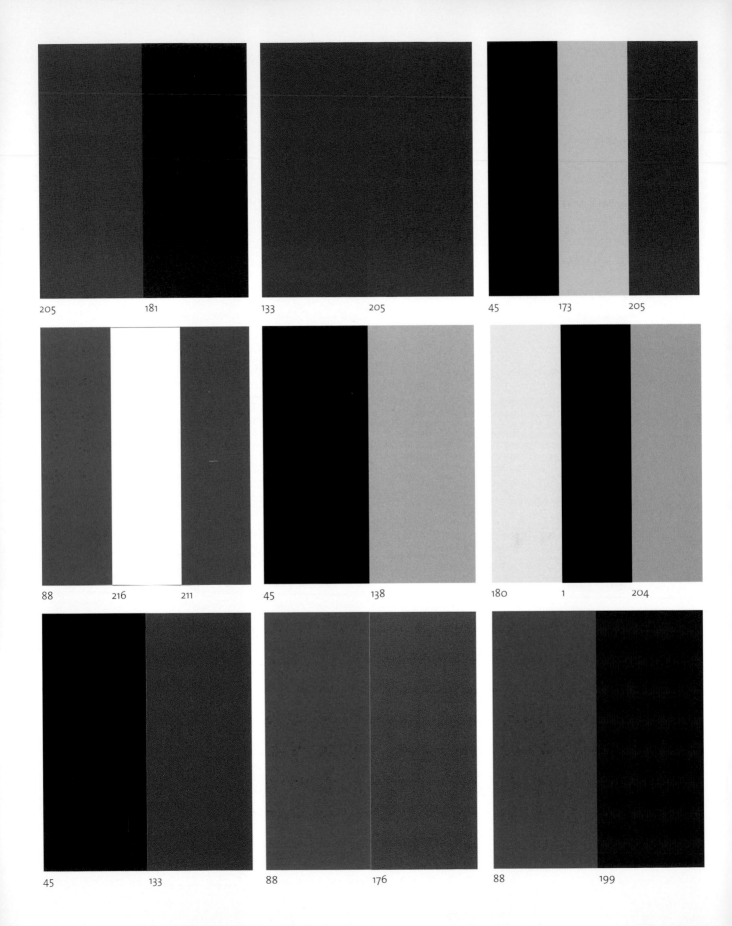

205   181   133   205   45   173   205

88   216   211   45   138   180   1   204

45   133   88   176   88   199

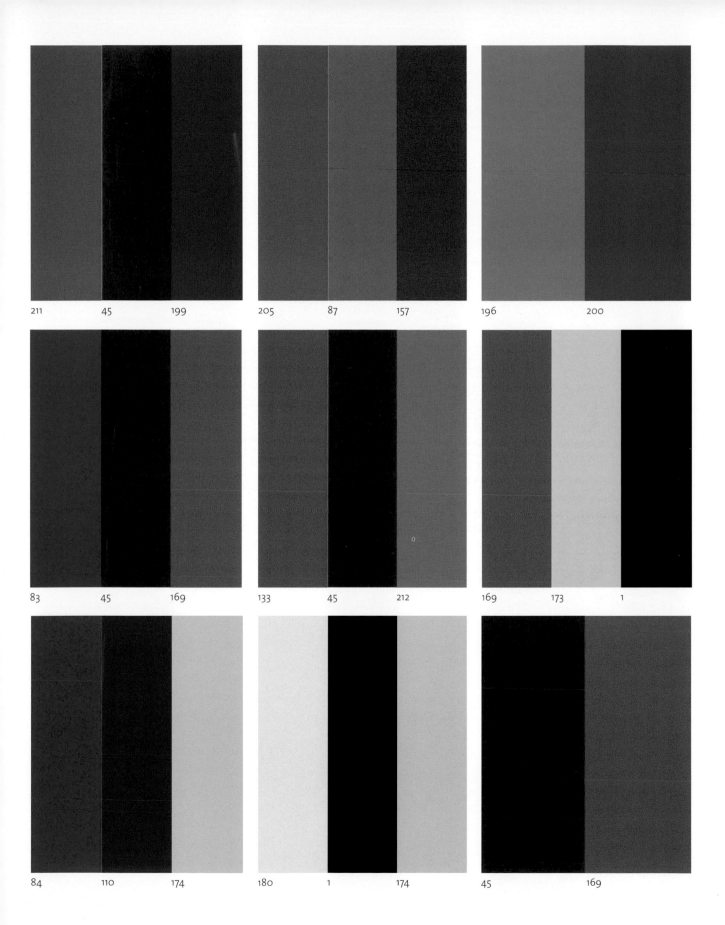

211   45   199

205   87   157

196   200

83   45   169

133   45   212

169   173   1

84   110   174

180   1   174

45   169

Calming

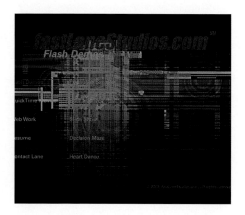

A significant benefit of using soothing colors on a web site is that people are able to look at them for prolonged periods. Fast Lane Studios, a design firm in the Bay Area, took a unique approach when choosing their site's color palette. "I started with a background image, but the colors were far too bright," says Lane Good of Fast Lane. He toned down the colors for a subtle effect. "I wanted colors that look as if they have a black gauze over them." The colors are muted and soft against an aggressive background and design, for an interesting combination of active image with soothing colors. The result is an intriguing, adventurous, abstract design that captures the mood of the work created at Fast Lane.

When designing Hawaii Seascapes, a web site for a company that creates custom coral reef aquariums, Frank Amodo, designer at RevaComm in Honolulu, looked to capture the tranquillity expressed in the products. "We wanted to create an atmosphere in which the user can experience the beautiful wonders that lie in the Hawaiian waters and that Hawaiian Seascapes re-creates." The rich colors were selected to simulate the Pacific Ocean. From the varied tones of blue to the subtle accent colors, the calming feeling exquisitely evokes the beauty of the undersea world.

HAWAII seascapes

about us | gallery | products & services | contact us | home

Hawaii Seascapes
is a company of people who
love nature and the sea.
Our work is a continuum
and an expression of
this love for the beauty
of life. We pride ourselves
in our creativity and
in producing results that
bring our clients
lasting pleasure.

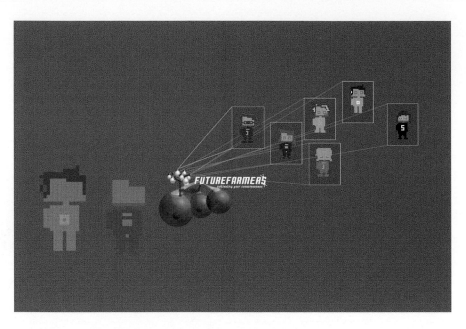

When Amy Franceschini was creating the site for Futurefarmers, her design firm in San Francisco, she wanted a soothing look. "This is where our work is shown. It must reflect us," she says. The soft colors were chosen to evoke a dreamy feeling. "I wanted the colors in the site to look as if there's a screen over everything," she says. From the soft yellows and beiges to the easy pinks and muted oranges, this site gives a strong calming feel, allowing the viewer a relaxing visual experience, and reflecting the feel of Futurefarmers itself. By using tints, the pages speak quietly to the viewer. The use of beige and browns allows for an almost neutral background and therefore ideal backdrop for her creative, unique, and memorable images. Futurefarmers cleverly demonstrates that effective design need not shout its colors. Tones that whisper may result in more compelling design.

45   46   88   136   118   116   130   136   115

88   136   45   136   128   116   136

116   88   144   114   81   116   173

118   136   139   144   159   144

180   94   166   180   169   174

77   1   152   163   44   110   136   1   110

43   163   75   130   166   175   44

121   1   159   108   87   109   65   1   73

86   102   79   166   164   44   137

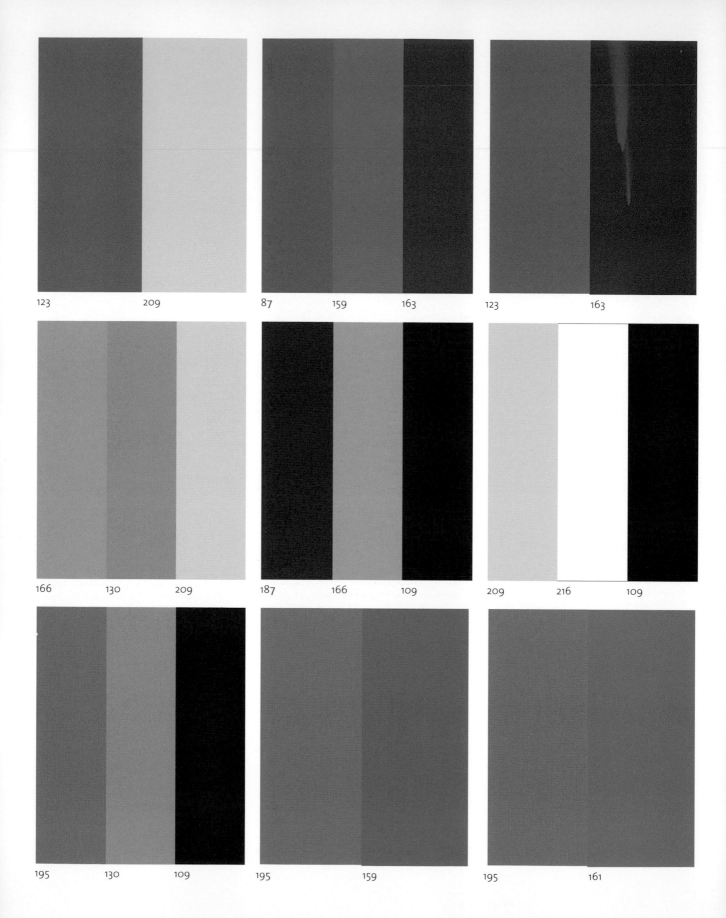

123   209

87   159   163

123   163

166   130   209

187   166   109

209   216   109

195   130   109

195   159

195   161

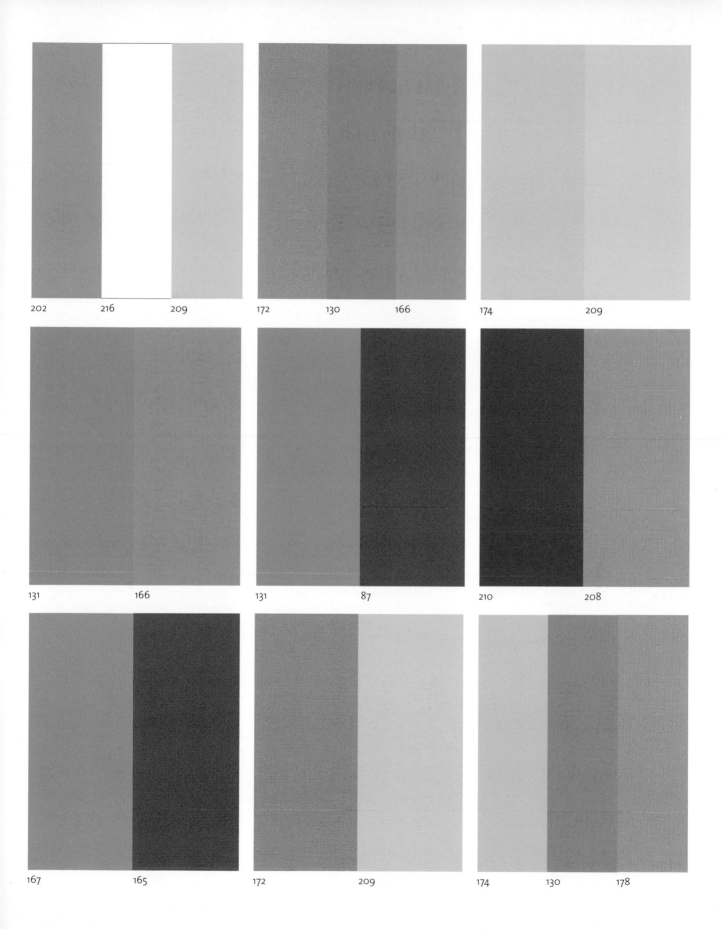

202　　　　216　　　　209　　　　172　　　130　　　166　　　　174　　　　209

131　　　　　166　　　　131　　　　87　　　　210　　　　208

167　　　　165　　　　172　　　　209　　　　174　　　130　　　178

Classic

To capture a feeling for ArtMuseum.net, the Intel-driven site developed to promote upcoming art exhibitions, Tim Barber at Rare Medium in San Francisco looked at the designs that were going on the site and chose classic colors to complement it. "When this site was created," he says, "the designers were becoming more inventive with technology. In this case, the screen begins quite spartan and becomes more lush as the user interacts with it." As the site was promoting an exhibition of American art, the creative team chose red and white to give the visitor a feeling for the celebration of the American Century. The visitor is drawn in as the colors grow deeper and more intense through use of the site. The classic colors, enhanced with clever use of interactivity, reinforce the sense of the traditional.

Dell, the Austin-based computer company, needed a site for their Japanese market. "They wanted a site for Japan, yet they wanted it to look non-Japanese. So we went for an American look," says Terry Green of twenty2product in San Francisco. The colors he chose for this design are traditional combinations plus deep browns and black. The color palette is strong and classic, allowing for an innovative design. The first page has concentric circles that are enhanced through the rich play of browns, beiges, and blacks over grays. The effect is both comforting, through the use of classic, dark colors, and challenging, as the familiar colors overlay the unfamiliar in the design.

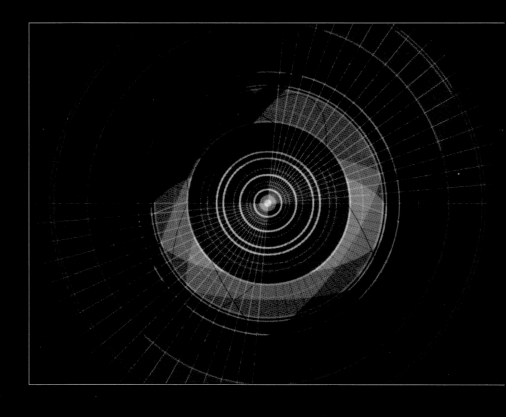

The other pages use muted colors to enhance and allow for more evocative designs. The blue, gray, and black combinations are familiar to the viewer, giving a sense of comfort. Offsetting these innately pleasing hues with off-center, innovative images makes the lines and arcs become more visible and intense. The typically corporate colors in this site are used to great effectiveness, allowing the subtle use of accent color and national identifiers to stand out. This subtlety of color extends through other pages. Secondary pages continue to employ repetition of imagery. The repetition of the characters and lines reinforces the complexity of the product to create an innovative backdrop and allow the Dell logo to stand out. This inventive mix of classic and non-traditional colors and imagery expands the reach of the Dell site, communicating both the reliability of Dell and its inventiveness—two attributes that have contributed to the company's success.

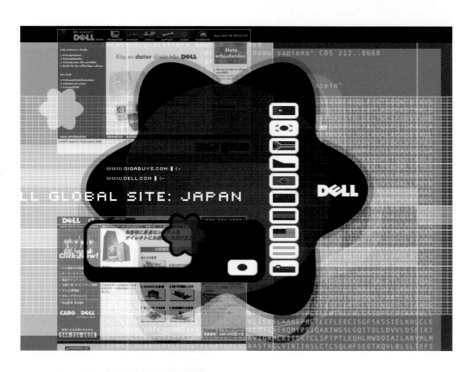

1   212

4   55   129

156   180   48

10   22

2   130   4

56   176   84

60   180   88

8   143   25

152   173   76

52   172   92   138   197   77   138   17

130   132   60   159   173   143   173   88

6   130   146   180   88   188   188   211   200

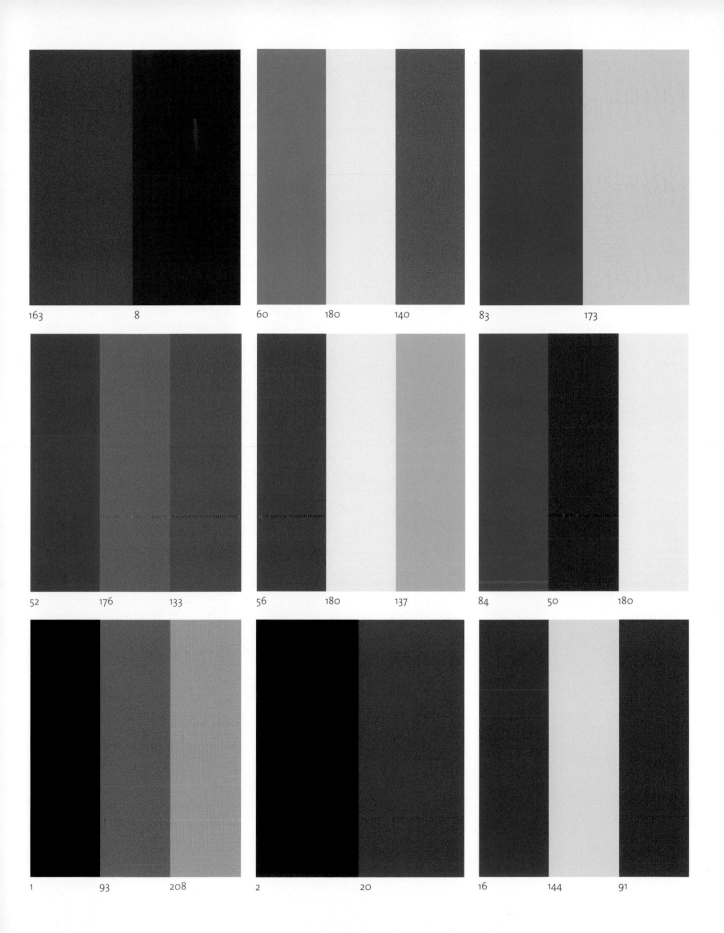

163   8   60   180   140   83   173

52   176   133   56   180   137   84   50   180

1   93   208   2   20   16   144   91

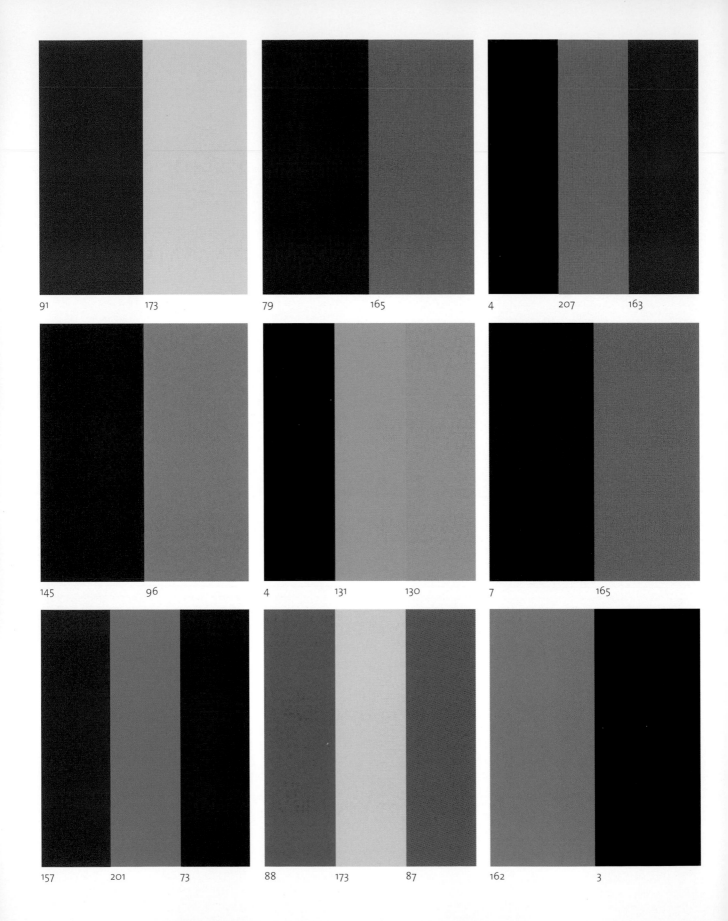

91   173

79   165

4   207   163

145   96

4   131   130

7   165

157   201   73

88   173   87

162   3

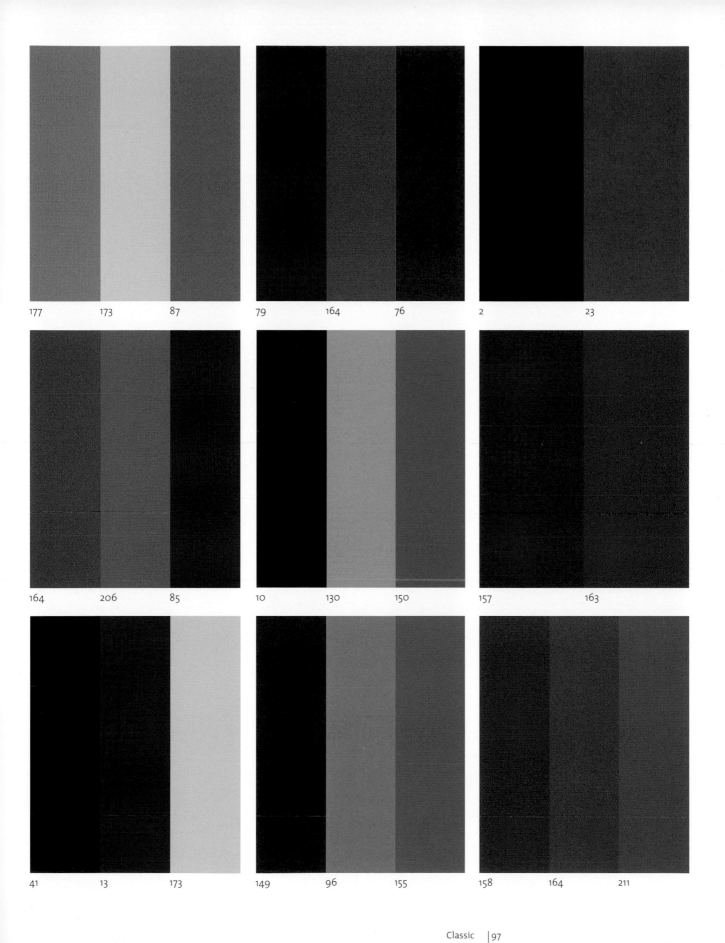

177   173   87

79   164   76

2   23

164   206   85

10   130   150

157   163

41   13   173

149   96   155

158   164   211

Bold

To capture boldness in a site, designers must select colors that complement designs without overwhelming them. The Fox Interactive site, created by Rare Medium in early 1999 to promote Fox's computer games, is a great example of boldness by design. "The direction was light, bright, bold, and exuberant," says Tim Barber, creative director. "We wanted a site that was fun, fresh, and full of energy." The colors were selected to appeal to the site's young audience—Generation Y or the younger Generation X. Orange and yellow are predominant. "We wanted the energy and boldness of the Playstation games," says Barber. The result is attitude and excitement with a memorable design and color palette.

The Unfurled site, designed by Terry Green at twenty2product in San Francisco, was created for a partnership between Yahoo! and MTV as a source for music. The challenge was to find a design and color palette that worked across these two companies, which have very different sensibilities. "We wanted a look that emulated a fanzine," says Green. The energy and boldness of the colors were supported by the cut-and-paste look of the design. The power of the outward spiral pulls out the bold reds, pinks, and yellows. The colors bring energy to the site and express its feeling of excitement.

unfURLed™

TERRA OBSCURA | ALL AROUND GOOD GUYS | TECHS-N-EFFECT | PRETTY IN PING | SMARTY RANTS | BELOW THE BELT | ENCYCLOPEDPHILES | INFINITE LINK | COME TOGETHER | U.R.O.S (UNIDENTIFIED POSING OBJECTS)

The energy of the colors is continued on the secondary pages. The purples highlight the name, with white acting as a light to suggest an arc or a curve. A deeply saturated red on another part of the page allows the brand to pop out, while challenging the balance of black, white, and purple. The blend of these two strong colors, black and red, with highlights of purple, yellow and white, brings a bold, unusual combination to the design. This vivacity is continued through the rest of the site. Solid, thick black lines contrast with purple concentric circles forming an off-center target. The repetition of images and lines along with the text and centered images continue the bold design statement. Beginning with vivid colors, Green has extended the feeling of the site through its pages to capture the mood in both color and texture, appealing to its target audience, the younger, more music-oriented Internet users.

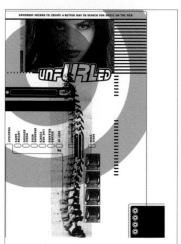

212   204   160   203   145   102   124

147   124   146   183   96   124   108

154   189   124   193   111   150   194   202

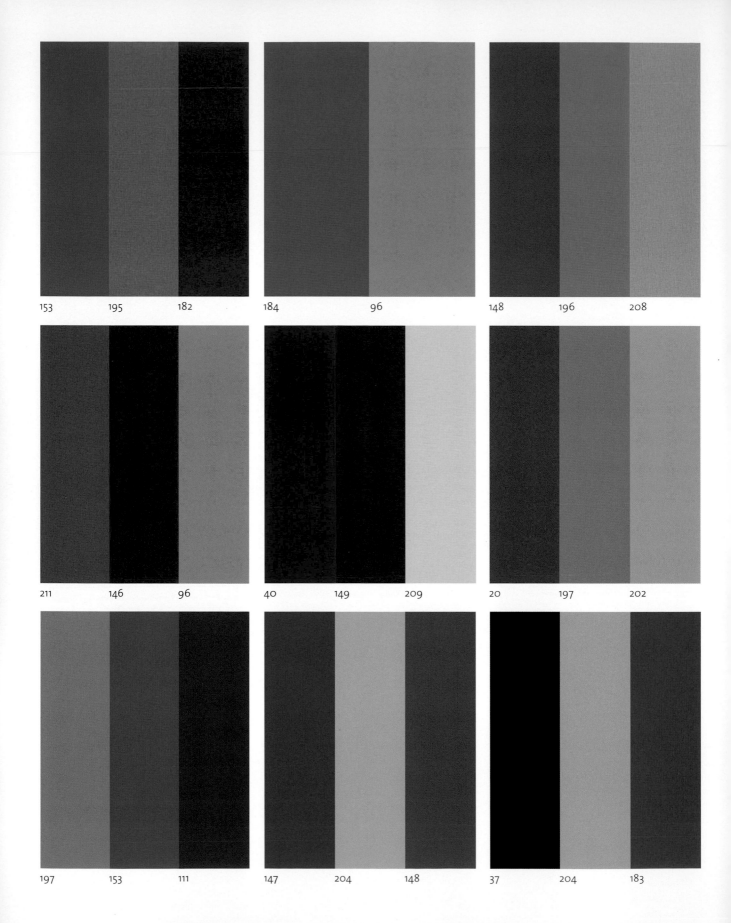

153   195   182

184   96

148   196   208

211   146   96

40   149   209

20   197   202

197   153   111

147   204   148

37   204   183

Color Harmony for the Web

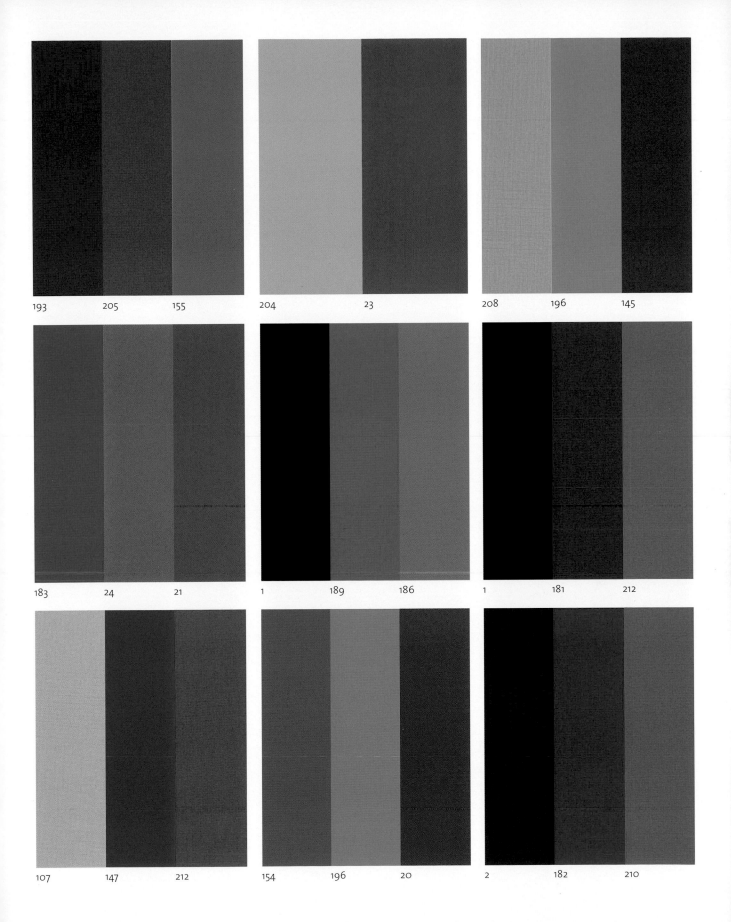

193 205 155

204 23

208 196 145

183 24 21

1 189 186

1 181 212

107 147 212

154 196 20

2 182 210

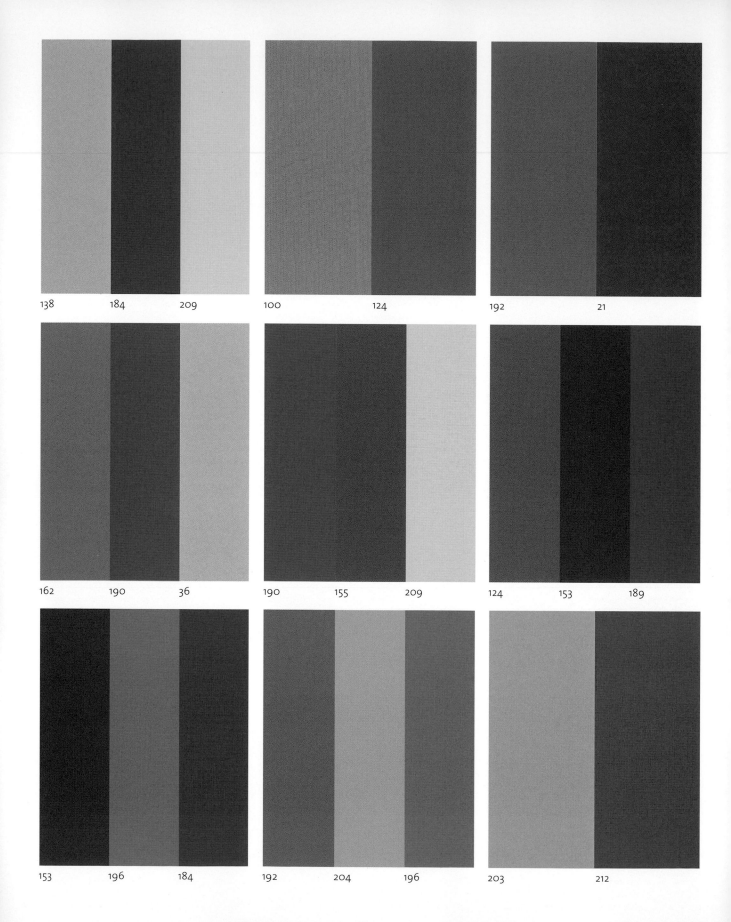

138   184   209

100   124

192   21

162   190   36

190   155   209

124   153   189

153   196   184

192   204   196

203   212

Color Harmony for the Web

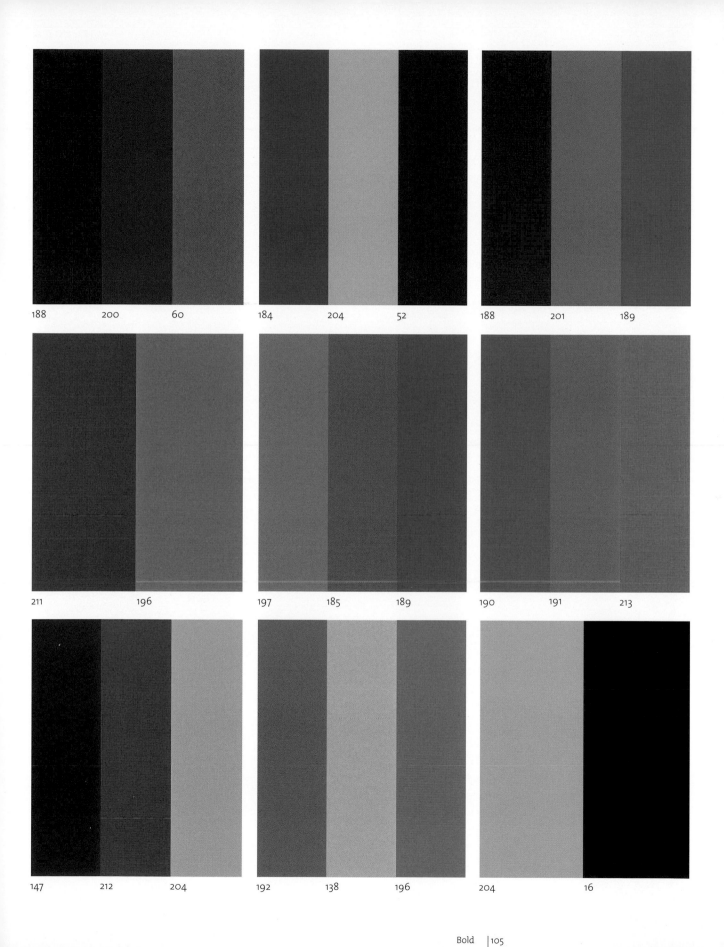

188　　　200　　　60　　　　184　　　204　　　52　　　　188　　　201　　　189

211　　　　　196　　　　197　　　185　　　189　　　　190　　　191　　　　213

147　　　212　　　204　　　　192　　　138　　　196　　　　204　　　　16

Subdued

Altpick.com is a source for people looking to hire illustrators, photographers, and other visual creatives, so the site design and colors needed to be appropriate for any of the thousands of images that could be selected for the home page. Here, the artwork itself is the star, so John Caserta, the site designer, chose colors that would complement but not detract from the images. The rich burgundy of the logo sits against the deep gray of the background. "We wanted to highlight the artwork. Anything other than subdued colors would detract from showcasing the work," says Caserta. This subtlety is continued across the secondary pages, where earthy highlight colors contribute to the quiet design. By choosing subdued colors, the visual designs stand out to better promote the artists who market their work through altpick.com.

When developing the site for PFA Architects, a commercial architectural firm in San Francisco, Chip Taylor, at M8BIUS Intermedia, began by visiting their office. "I looked at their designs and their choice of carpet, textiles, and wall covering. They used a muted palette. It was subdued and pleasing to the eye," says Taylor. The architects wanted the site to be approachable and complete. "We found a depth in the simplicity," says Taylor, as demonstrated by his choice of subtle blues and greens. By carrying the color palette from the architects' office to their web site, Taylor was able to complete the circle, giving potential clients a strong sense of the firm's work while creating a pleasing, professional web site.

Paul Finch & Associates, P.C. 3550 buckner blvd., virginia beach, va 23456 tel: 757 471 0537 fax: 757 471 4205

Architects & Planners

WELCOME
to our Web site

Paul Finch & Associates, P.C. is an architecture and planning firm located in Virginia Beach, Virginia. We specialize in healthcare facilities, interior wayfinding, office buildings, and interior design.

Please select from the menu above to navigate to those subject pages. Inside PF&A will explain the inner workings and introduce the people behind our company. Browse through a selection of our design portfolio in Projects. Our Newsletter, to which you may subscribe, is the ultimate off-line resource for all things new and exciting in the world of architecture and healthcare design. Finally, do not hesitate to get in touch with us on the Contact page. Should you like to come back to this page, select Home.

If you missed or would like to replay our Flash intro movie, click here. Remember, you will need the Macromedia Flash plug-in for your 4.0+ browser.

The Cymatix site was created in 1998 by Darren Campeau, art director of Campeau Communications in San Francisco. Cymatix creates robotic devices, so Campeau wanted to convey a manufacturing sensibility—and, broadly, to translate the images and feeling of the company to its design. Says Campeau, "We wanted a site that was pleasing and compelling but, given the nature of the product, not too dry." By cleverly mixing black and white and retro images over subdued blues and grays, Campeau created a site that evokes tradition and experience while providing a visually subtle experience. The result is a design that speaks of continuity and expertise in an innovative manner.

43   85   208

208   207

1   208   7

2   207   79

201   209   208

80   201   200

28   143   144

140   208

85   20

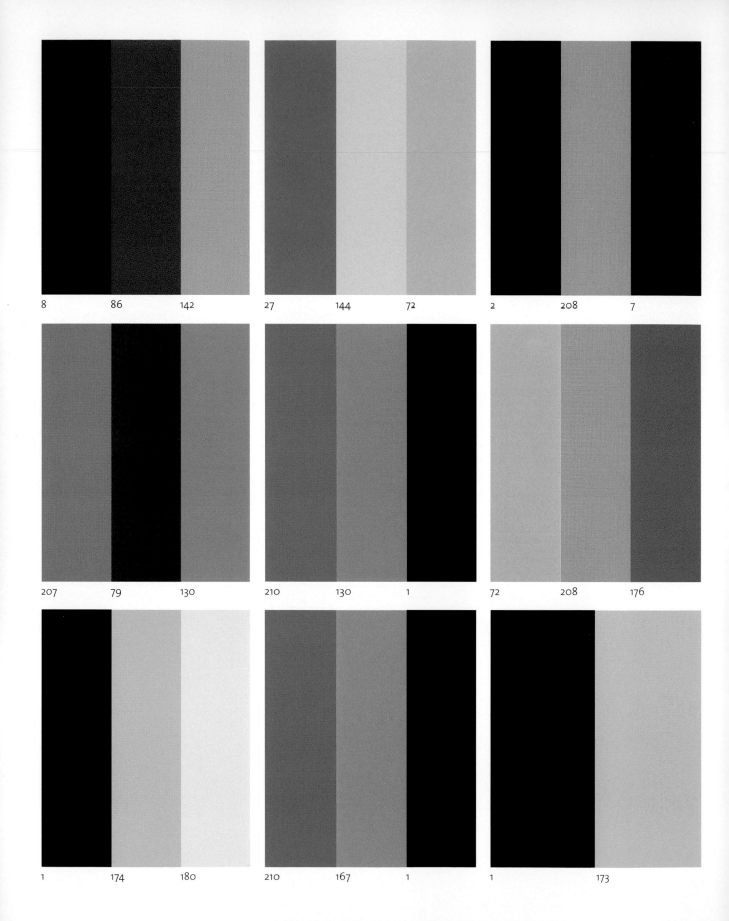

8   86   142

27   144   72

2   208   7

207   79   130

210   130   1

72   208   176

1   174   180

210   167   1

1   173

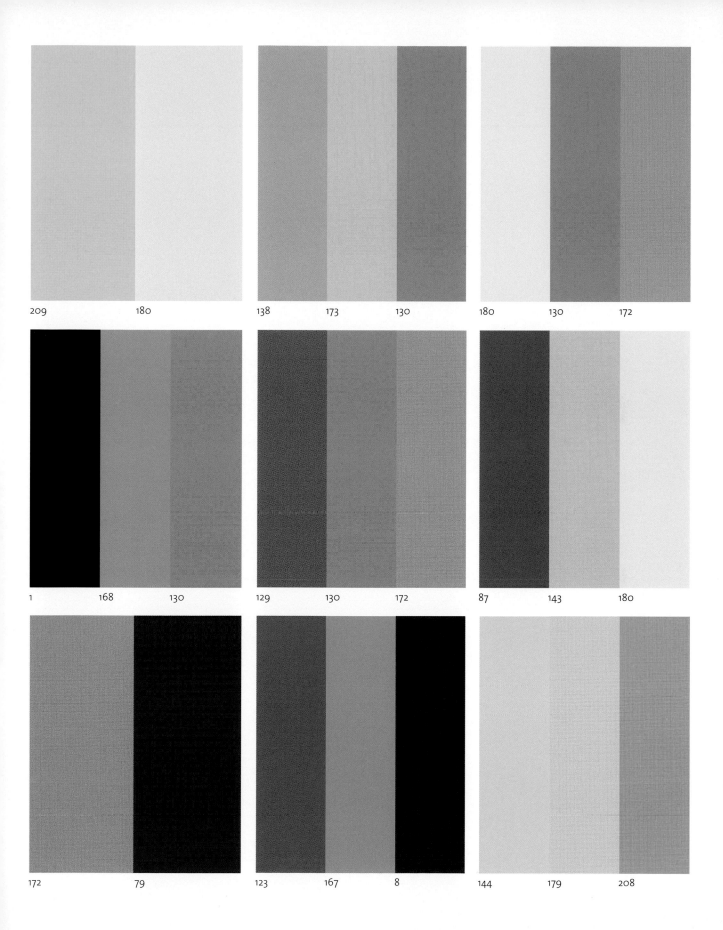

209   180   138   173   130   180   130   172

1   168   130   129   130   172   87   143   180

172   79   123   167   8   144   179   208

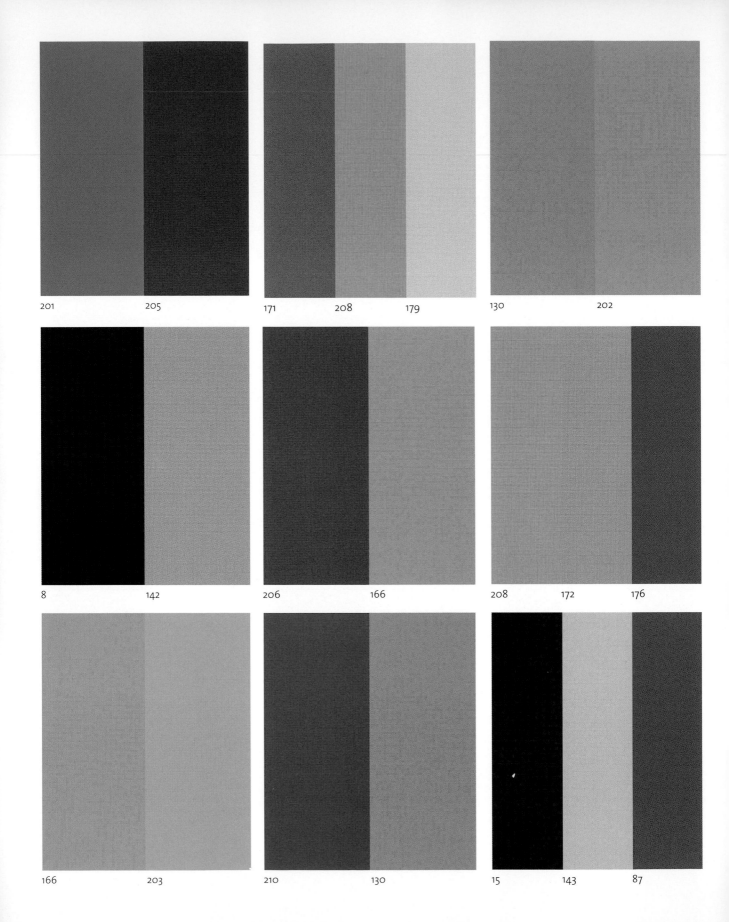

201   205

171   208   179

130   202

8   142

206   166

208   172   176

166   203

210   130

15   143   87

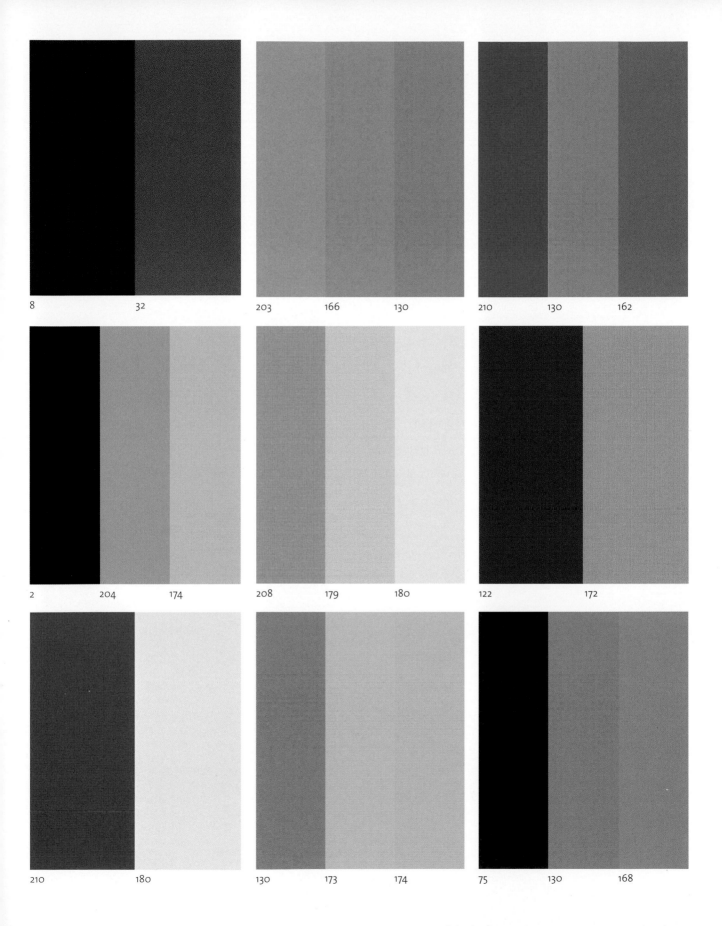

8   32

203   166   130

210   130   162

2   204   174

208   179   180

122   172

210   180

130   173   174

75   130   168

Refreshing

The Teak for Life section of the Smith and Hawken site was created by Webb Design in San Francisco. Smith and Hawken wanted to capture the refreshment of outdoor living while highlighting a new line of furniture. "We used the fullest oranges and greens with muted accent colors to bring out the exhilarating feeling of being outdoors," says Kim Webb, creative director. The site's saturated color palette evokes fresh air; the subtle highlight colors add a refreshing touch while maintaining the calm feeling associated with Smith and Hawken products.

Other sections offer content for avid gardeners and would-be green thumbs.

"We wanted to design the What's New section like a periodical, with color enhancing the page," says Webb. Smith and Hawken had a definite concept for this page. While the major areas on the site share a focused, earthy palette, this section needed a wider color range to reflect the seasonality and renewal of the content. For the June image, Webb chose a bright purple to frame the issue topic: edible flowers. Bringing the beauty of the garden to the page makes for a memorable design. The refreshing colors complement both the image and the muted green of the Smith and Hawken corporate palette. The floral tones capture the excitement of a color-drenched garden while allowing for an easily read and navigated site.

SEARCH

VIEW BASKET
CHECKOUT
CUSTOMER SERVICE

Smith & Hawken   SHOP   RESOURCES   STORES   JUNE

TEAK FOR LIFE | EDIBLE FLOWERS | GARDEN STRUCTURES | SUMMER MENU

edible flowers

by Rachel Raphael

My mother is a master chef. Although my adult taste buds are thankful for that now, I struggled with her exotic menus as a child. Mussels and rabbit were typical entrees on the dinner table, when all I longed for were the simple things: fishsticks, french fries, and — on a daring evening — noodles slathered in butter. I distinctly remember the night that flowers appeared in my salad. (It was the same evening that my beloved ranch dressing was replaced by an acerbic vinaigrette.) Flowers? No way. Weren't they poisonous? Clearly, my mom's culinary journey had wandered off the flavor and safety map.

My mother is a master chef. Although my adult taste buds are thankful for that now, I struggled with her exotic menus as a child. Mussels and rabbit were typical entrees on the dinner table, when all I longed for were the simple things: fishsticks, french fries, and — on a daring

Rachel's Favorite Edibles

Anise Hyssop (*Agastache foeniculum*): If you like licorice and fennel, then this is the flower for you. Anise hyssop lends itself to both sweet and savory dishes.

Borage (*Borago officinalis*): Warm blue tones and a cucumber flavor make borage a must for edible flower enthusiasts. It's gorgeous tossed in salads with nasturtiums.

Daylily (*Hemerocallis*): You can feast on all parts of this plant, but the flowers are my favorite. Flavor depends on color, with pale shades on the sweet side and dark shades on the vegetal side. Use daylily blooms in Chinese dishes, like stir fries and hot and sour soup.

Johnny-Jump-Up (*Viola tricolor*): Romantic hues and a mild mint flavor make this the quintessential edible flower for lettuce and fruit salads.

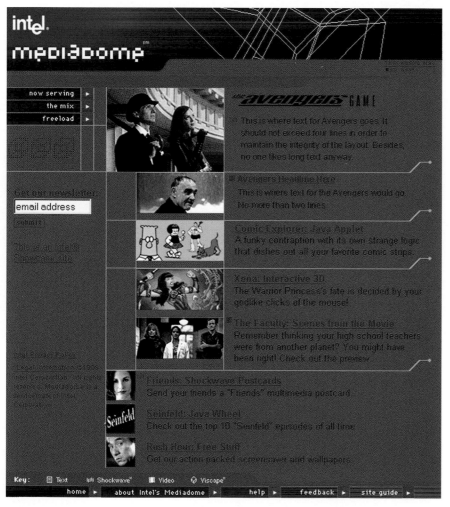

The Intel MediaDome site was created in 1998 by Rare Medium as a joint venture with Intel and CNET. It began as a means of developing partnerships with film, recording, artistic, and web-based entertainment companies to create multimedia experiences that showcased the power of the Intel processor. The target audience is teenagers and college students. "We chose colors that were cool in temperature and precise, and we had to work with the specific Intel blue. We continued this Intel branding through the site to create a unique visual experience with brand equity for a true sense of ownership," says Tim Barber, creative director. The various hues of bright, clean green are a vivid, inviting background for the content-rich nature of the site. From new movies to popular television shows and recently released CDs, this site captured the freshness of new media in its design. The rich accent colors contribute to the refreshing feel of the site. By selecting colors that provide a vivid contrast to the Intel blue, Rare Medium created a site that is fun to use and evocative of its exciting, media-based content.

9   13   16   214   23   102   202

55   138   66   211   29   162   166   147

102   204   208   81   154   196   216   131

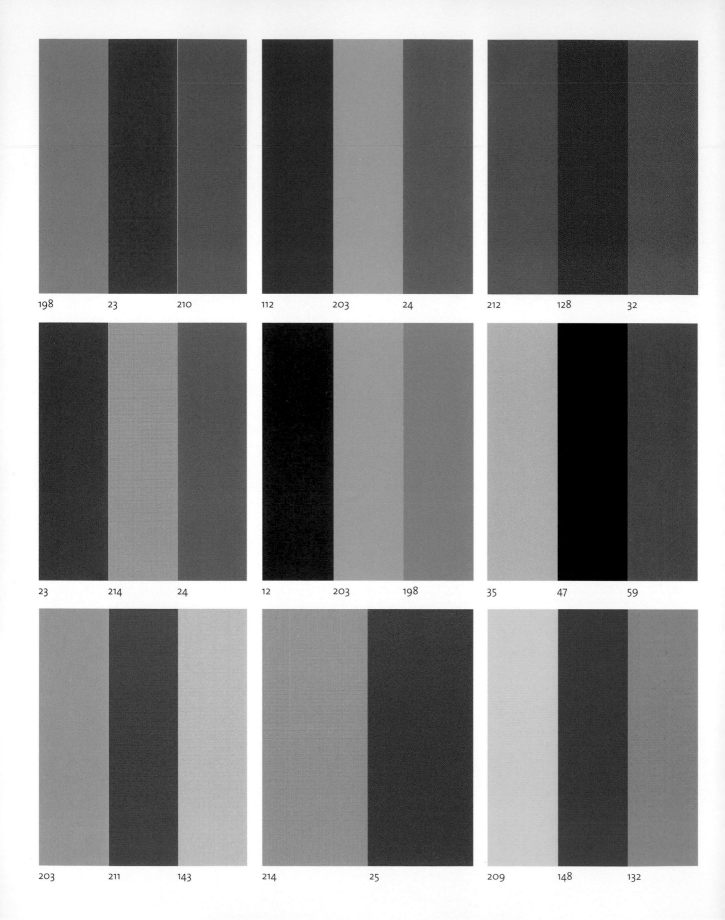

| 198 | 23 | 210 | | 112 | 203 | 24 | | 212 | 128 | 32 |

| 23 | 214 | 24 | | 12 | 203 | 198 | | 35 | 47 | 59 |

| 203 | 211 | 143 | | 214 | 25 | | 209 | 148 | 132 |

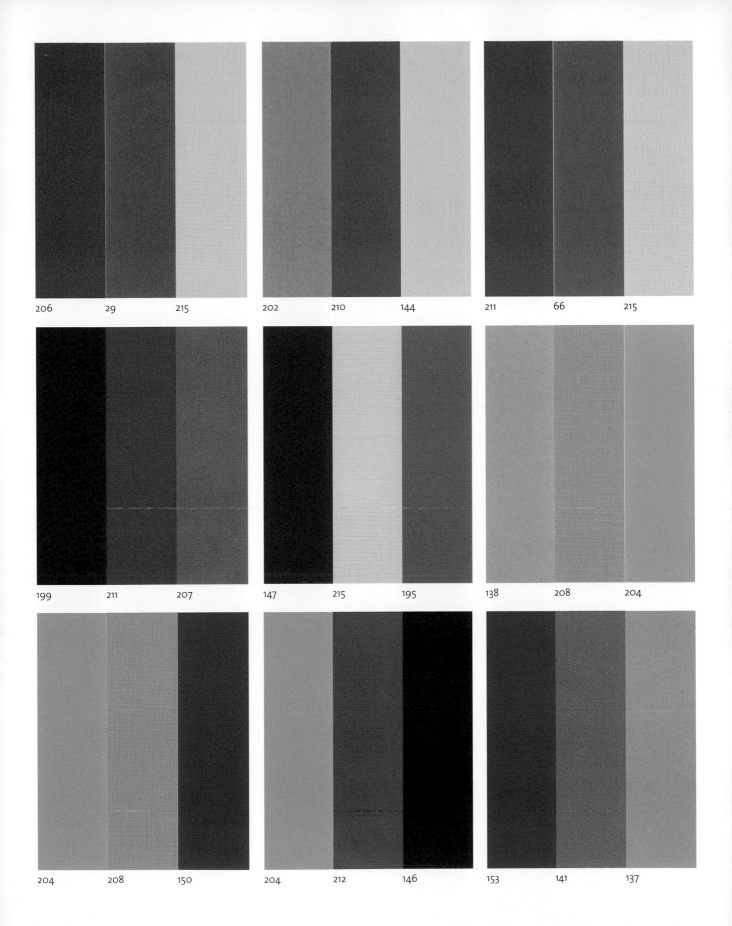

206   29   215   202   210   144   211   66   215

199   211   207   147   215   195   138   208   204

204   208   150   204   212   146   153   141   137

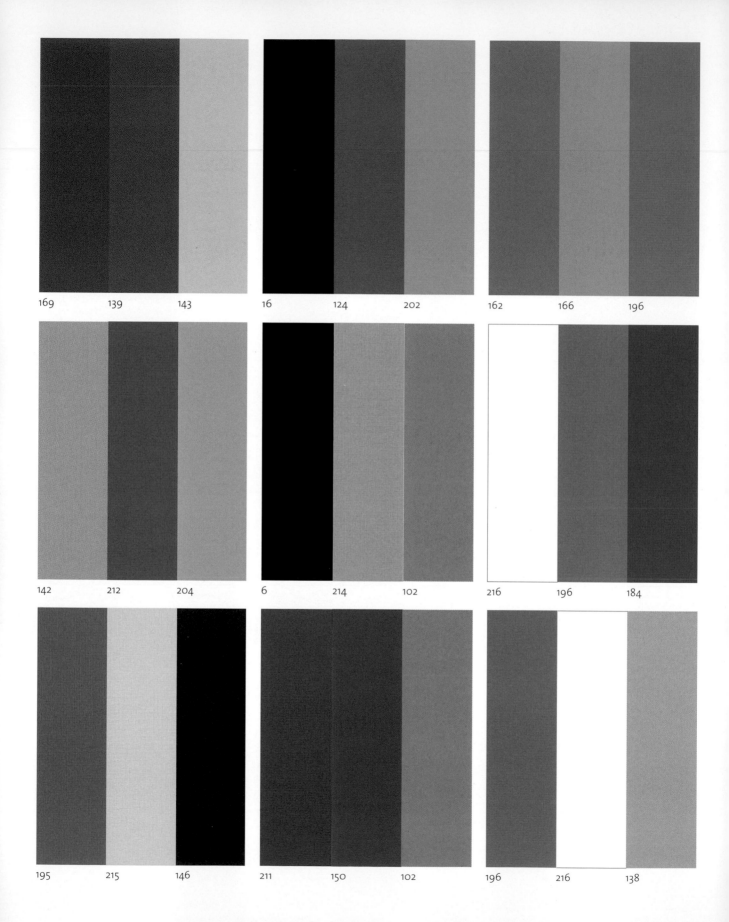

169   139   143   16   124   202   162   166   196

142   212   204   6   214   102   216   196   184

195   215   146   211   150   102   196   216   138

Color Harmony for the Web

90   138   184   215   142   138   196   216   148

210   147   131   202   210   148   64   60   36

91   138   141   203   211   147   216   196

Aggressive

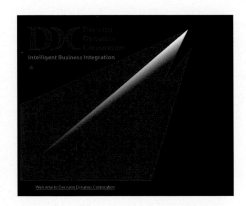

Decision Dynamix was developed in mid-1999 by Joshua Jacobson. The technology company enhances databases so they work faster and have more memory. "The president of the company said that he loved Ferrari red," says Jacobson, "so I took that idea and went for a fast, aggressive look." He focused on capturing a sense of speed in the design. "The black was the perfect color to offset the red," he says, "with a white highlight to evoke a razor-sharp edge." On the secondary pages, the red continues as the background frame on a white page to make the content easy to read. With the rich, aggressive colors, Jacobson created a site that contributes to the brand image of the company.

When designing the site for RockShox, a leading manufacturer of suspension devices for mountain biking, in 1999, Terry Green at twenty2product in San Francisco wanted to capture the dynamic nature of the product. A grid index maps all RockShox's suspension products by application, type, name, and cost and outlines how the products relate. In this way, customers know where each item fits into the product line and can avoid suboptimal upgrades. Color and design enable consumers to navigate simply through what otherwise would be a confusing list of products. The vivid oranges, reds, and yellows of the home page make for a dynamic landing page, signifying the energy of the product in use and the excitement of the sport.

The aggressiveness of color is continued through the rest of the RockShox design. Bold, rich tones complement the product-centered design. From the secondary pages, which are infused with purple, to the deep greens on other pages, the excitement of the product and its use is maintained. The rich use of color makes the RockShox design particularly successful at conveying its image and message. Images on secondary pages continue the excitement. A grid system turns colors into a structured image. Some of the oranges and greens used on previous pages are repeated, providing a continuity through a vividly different design. The sky blue at the edges of the page brings a calm surrounding to an otherwise startlingly accented page. Throughout the entire RockShox design, Green has taken powerful imagery and coupled it with bold choices of color, to create imagery that's as memorable as it is unique.

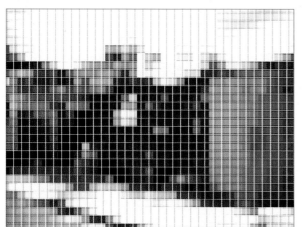

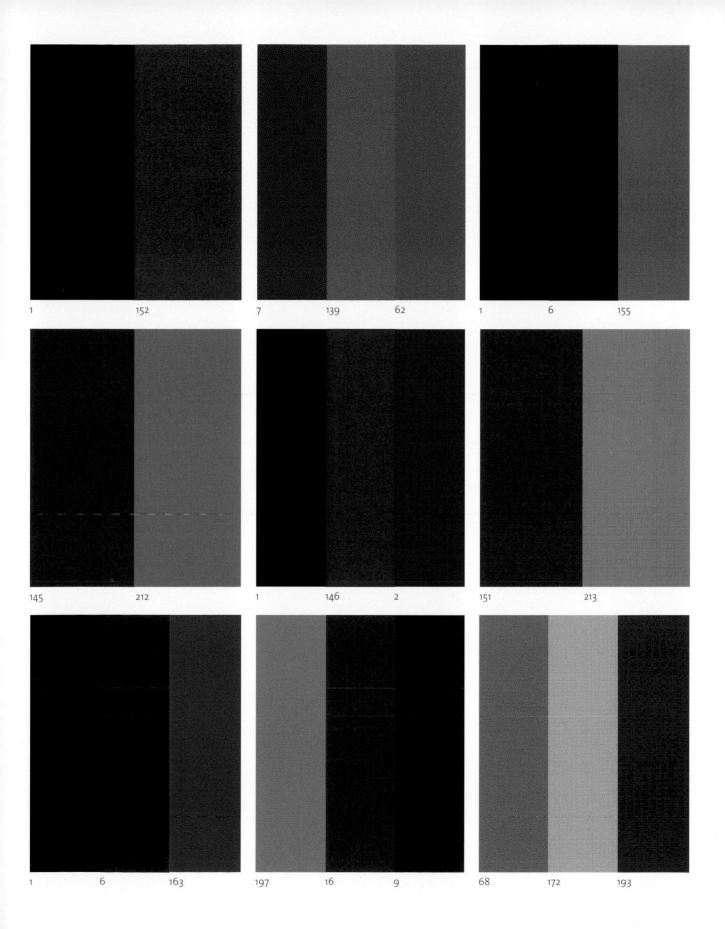

1   152

7   139   62

1   6   155

145   212

1   146   2

151   213

1   6   163

197   16   9

68   172   193

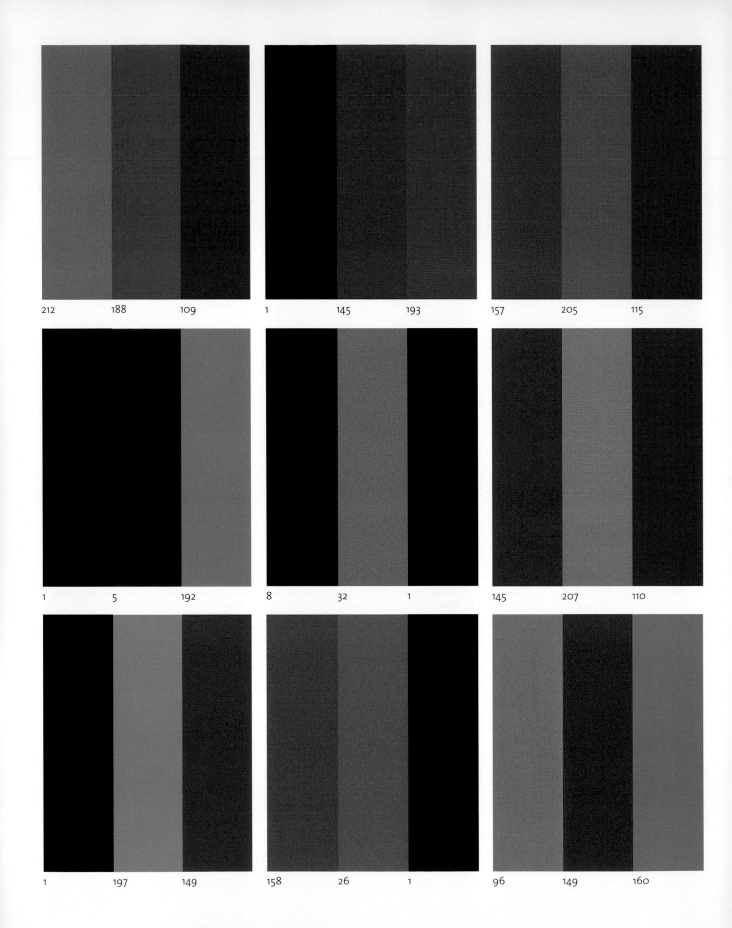

212	188	109	1	145	193	157	205	115
1	5	192	8	32	1	145	207	110
1	197	149	158	26	1	96	149	160

1   6   28   96   153   160   86   30

1   17   149   153   160   81   1   6   184

117   147   89   1   130   188   2   148

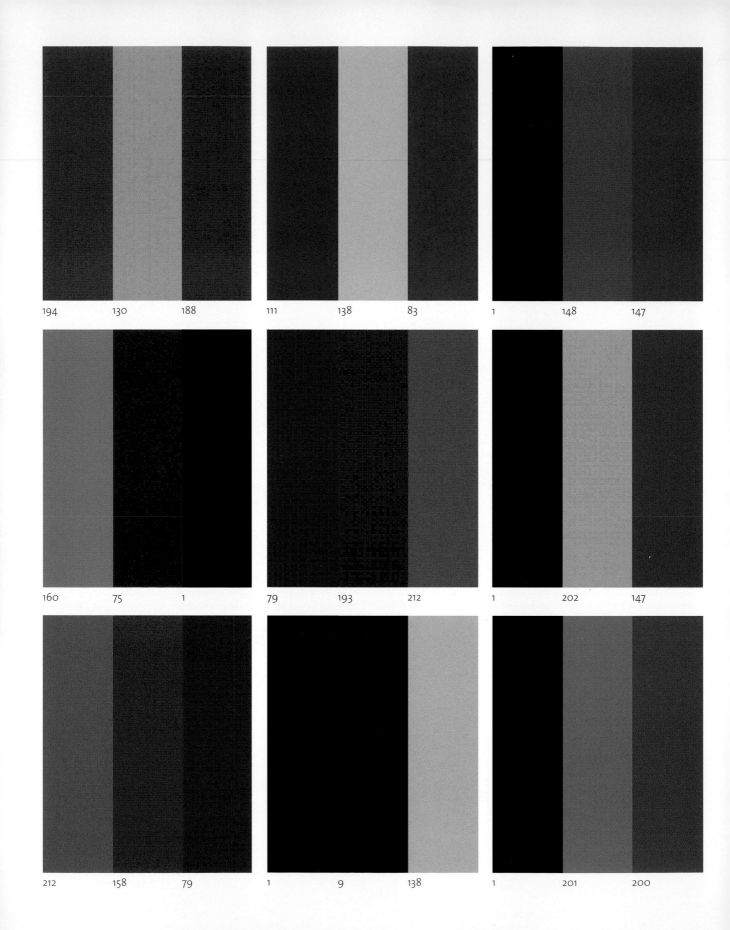

194   130   188

111   138   83

1   148   147

160   75   1

79   193   212

1   202   147

212   158   79

1   9   138

1   201   200

Color Harmony for the Web

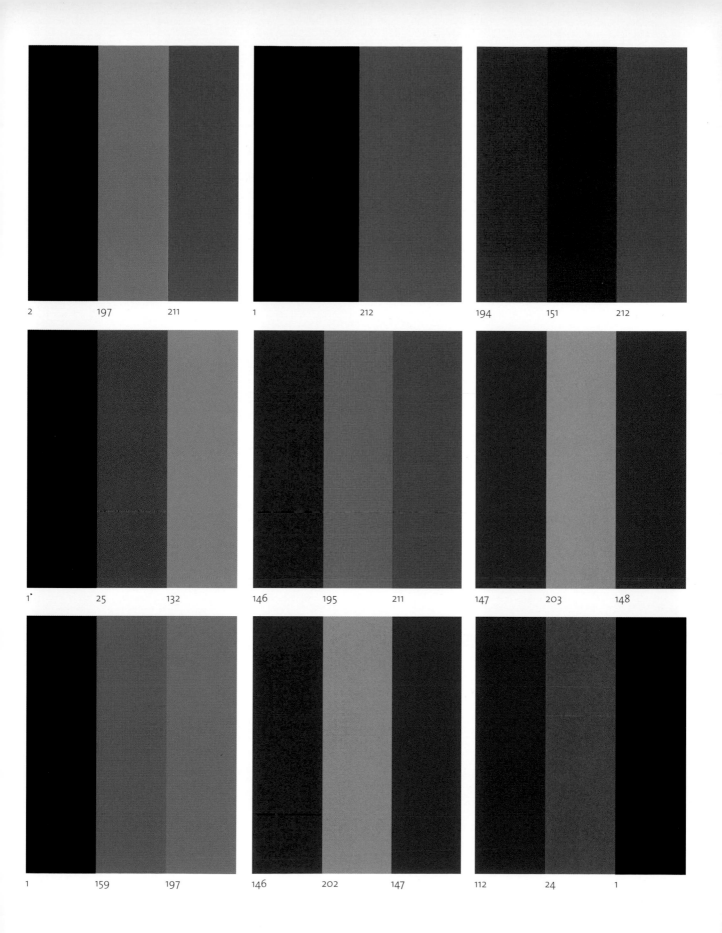

Friendly

Discussions.com was designed in 1999. The challenge facing the creative team at Terrascope was to give a face to the website. Because this is a community-based discussion site, Terrascope needed to create a friendly, approachable design and color palette. "The different topics and sections have different colors," says Bill Dunlap, creative director at Terrascope. "The community section is playful, with bright primary colors, which are soft and welcoming." Terrascope also used arcs and curves, rather than corners, to continue the soft feel. By creating a friendly community-based section, Terrascope gave discussions.com the interface they need to evoke the sense of comfort and accessibility critical for the company.

When developing the MCI corporate store site in 1998, Joshua Jacobson was able to move the telecom company away from a traditional image to a more personable look. The color palette was a large part of the success of this design. The site was created as an incentive program for MCI's employees. "We needed to give the site the MCI corporate identity but also make it fun, accessible, and exciting," Jacobson says. He added bright, highly saturated colors to MCI's corporate blue, orange, and white to put an exciting, friendly face on the company's site. The effect is welcoming and sociable, perfect for an employee incentive site.

MCI Collection 1998

MCI WORLDCOM items now available in Holiday Collection and Fall Rewards.

75% Off Final Sale!

All merchandise discounted from price listed on web. Discount given at confirmation of order at time of call.

Place your order TODAY!
1-800-969-6207

Welcome to the latest MCI Collection. Whether shopping for rewards for your team or treating yourself, the MCI collection has something everyone will love. Enjoy!

Holiday Collection

Wearable Collection

Event/Desk Collection

Executive/ Gifts

Fall Rewards

How to Order ⊛   Our Satisfaction Guarantee ⊛

Site Produced by **Wood Associates**. Web Development & Design by **OMIX**.

The colors and design needed to work throughout the year, so the inside pages continue the palette of the first page, with seasonal colors added to the range of tones. The pages begin with a fun, friendly feel, then expand to reflect the particular offerings. "The items offered were part of an ongoing collection," says Jacobson. The hues he selected evolved throughout the year, to highlight the changing products. The box design was chosen to give structure to the page and to make updating the product offerings more practical and efficient. The colors change across products, rather than across the pages themselves. This design structure lends far more flexibility to the site, allowing the MCI employee incentive program to update the selections when necessary without disturbing the site's overall look and feel. The strong color palette even aided the product photographer. When shooting the products for the site, the photographer was able to match the background colors of the product shots to contribute to the continuity of the site, so whenever the site is updated, it maintains its fresh, friendly accessible feel.

6   211   91

205   97

119   25

153   211   138

201   211   188

160   202   192

202   209   184

190   203   204

24   211   161

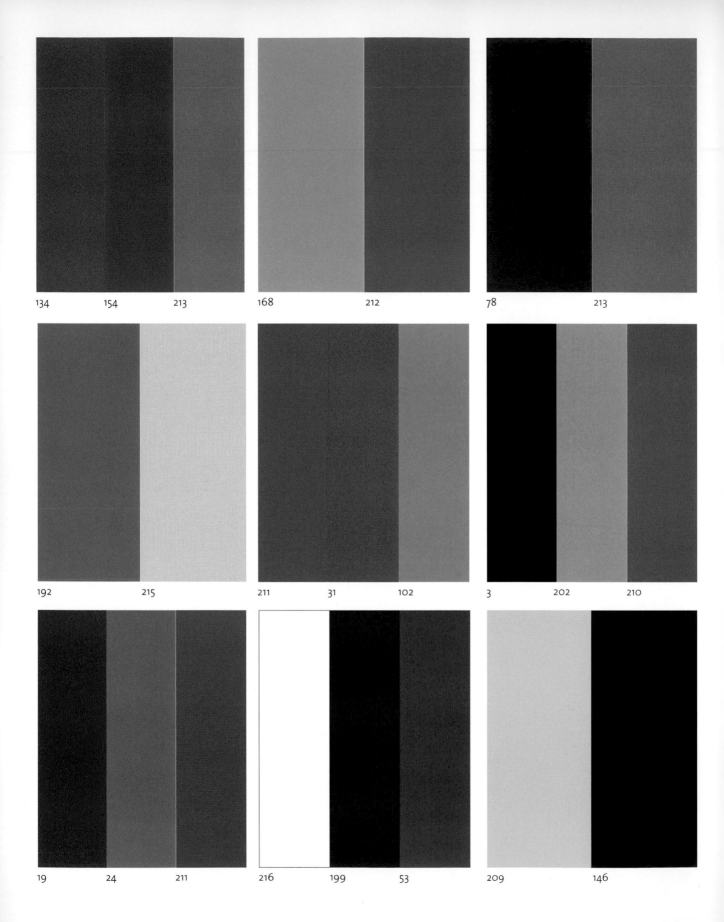

134   134   154   213

168   212

78   213

192   215

211   31   102

3   202   210

19   24   211

216   199   53

209   146

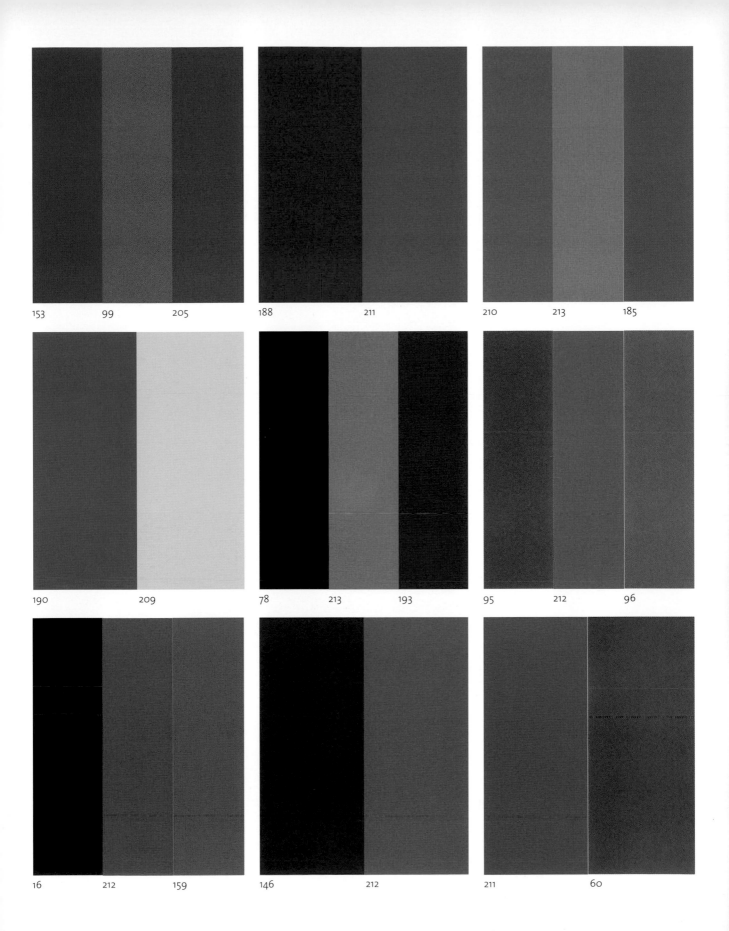

153   99   205   188   211   210   213   185

190   209   78   213   193   95   212   96

16   212   159   146   212   211   60

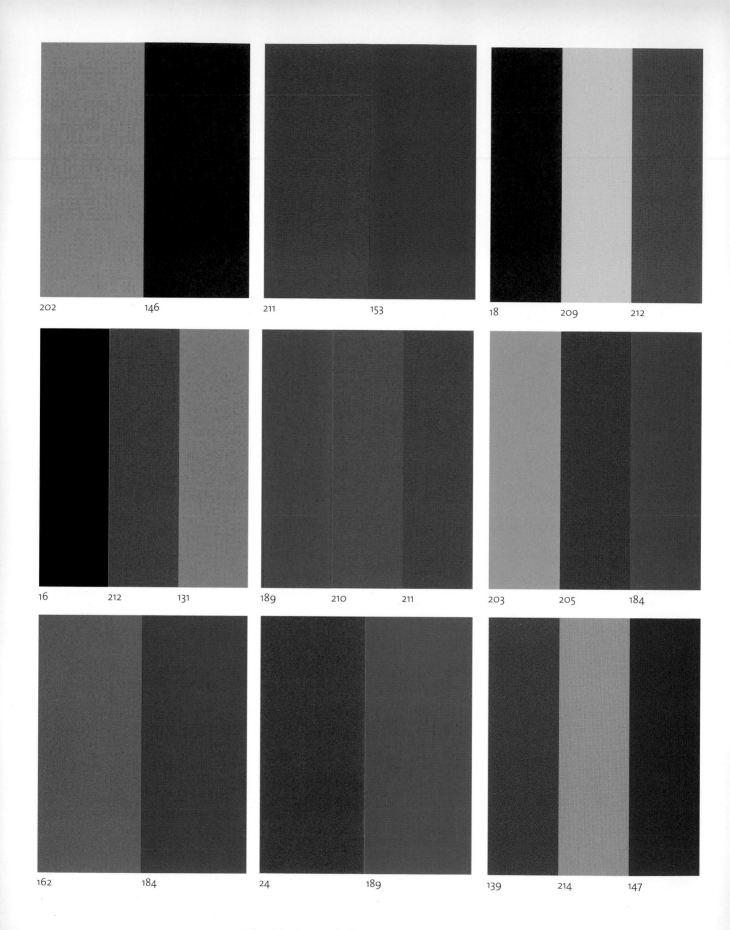

202   146   211   153   18   209   212

16   212   131   189   210   211   203   205   184

162   184   24   189   139   214   147

Color Harmony for the Web

212   162   152   211   159   160   211

3   212   139   193   213   196   212

193   213   91   211   199   196   209   212

Vibrant

When looking to create their own web site, DNA Visual Business Solutions of Chicago knew they wanted to reflect the creativity and fun that go into their work. "The design needed to speak to what DNA does," says Karen Shields, creative director. Their effective use of color is a large part of communicating their creativity. The text is made appealing and inviting by color. The site continues its friendly feel with large type that, with the colored text, is compelling and easy to read. This page in particular demonstrates beautifully how an otherwise white text on a black background can be brought to life with the right choice of color. "We wanted the site to look organic. We also wanted to convey the scientific side of what we do, and infuse it with warmth and inviting colors." By choosing rich colors, such as deep reds, DNA was able to create the energy that they wanted in their home page.

The tone of the colors is continued on the secondary pages. The Contact Us page enhances the approachability of the home page while introducing a deeply rich yellow-orange into the palette. This vibrancy lends an exquisite simplicity to the design of the site, contributing to its attained goals of being approachable, inviting, energetic, and fiery—all terms that describe the firm itself.

About DNA
Solutions
Portfolio
Contact Us

contact us

Directions
From:
O'Hare International Airport
Chicago, Illinois

In 1999, when RevaComm, a web design firm in Hawaii, created their own site, they wanted to capture a rich, energetic feel. The palette is vibrant with contrasting tones, the choice of which was inspired by the colors used to decorate the studio. One of the challenges facing Todd Masui, the designer at RevaComm, was to use just the right shades for the secondary pages. "Finding colors that work on the subpages was difficult, especially when limited to web-safe colors," he says. He began with the image of the rippling leaf pattern on RevaComm's logo. The top left corner is deeply textured, delivering vibrant colors to give depth to the image. From there, he selected the rich tones that make this site so memorable. Bright green is chosen as the highlight color against the deep purple and exquisite blue. The bright yellow that evolves from the orange in the top left corner suggests the warmth of the Hawaiian sun. When met with the defined horizontal line over a rich sea blue color, the effect is equally enlivening and slightly calming, as the effect is of the sun over the deep blue sea. The color intensity of this site, along with its texture and inventive use of lines and curves, beautifully demonstrates RevaComm's creativity and the vibrancy in the design firm.

5   161   165   18   164   23   43   163   211

162   155   210   3   162   163   6   166   203

16   164   12   9   165   145   18   166   160

15   164   172

24   160   168

1   169   33

4   172   36

7   163   1

16   172   212

24   172   40

1   173   41

3   174   190

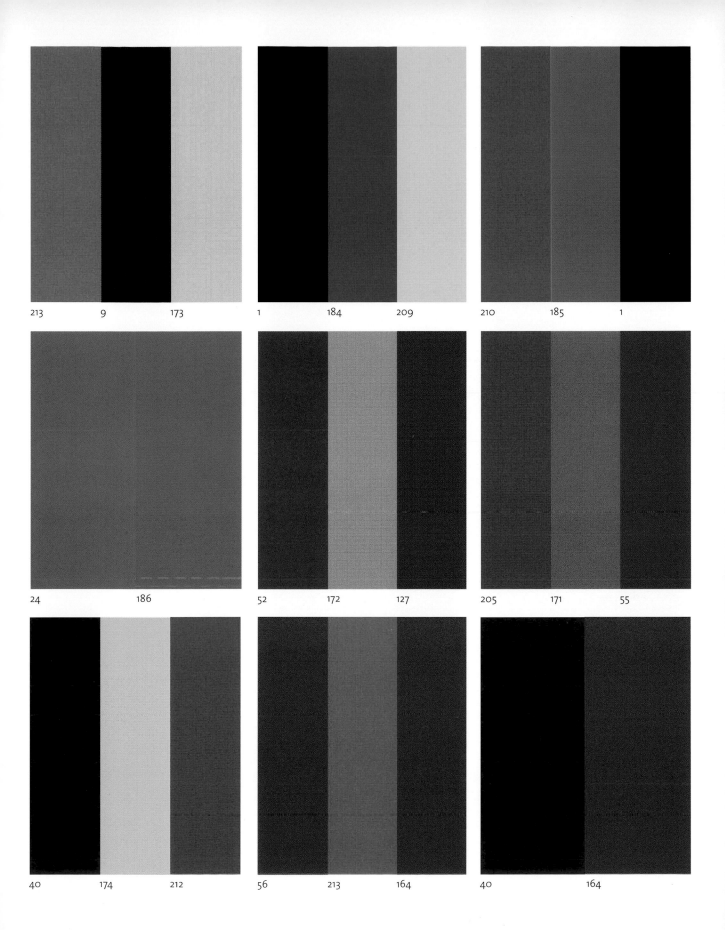

213   9   173

1   184   209

210   185   1

24   186

52   172   127

205   171   55

40   174   212

56   213   164

40   164

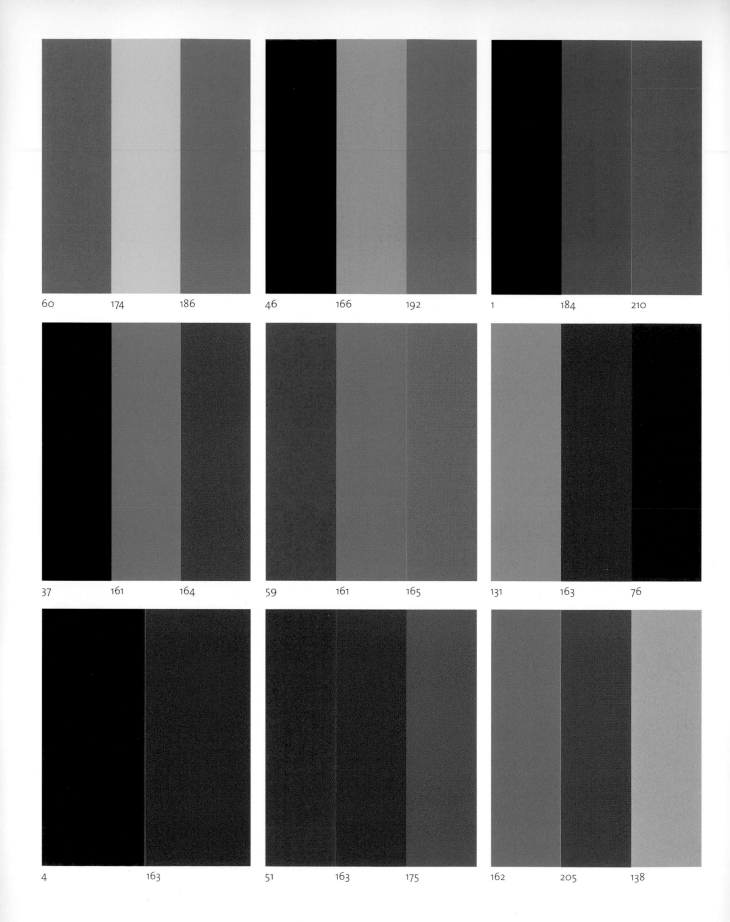

60   174   186

46   166   192

1   184   210

37   161   164

59   161   165

131   163   76

4   163

51   163   175

162   205   138

60   162

166   163   168

147   166   203

16   192   164

205   172   60

36   164

205   173   33

162   174   163

18   191   164

Professional

The site for uRreal, which creates real-time, collaborative e-commerce solutions and whose product is currently being embraced by the real estate market, uses colors that evoke professionalism. The color blue has long been associated with company logos. The trust and security inspired by the constancy of the sky make shades of blue popular in commercial design. Luke Desantos, designer, was looking for a professional yet friendly and accessible color palette. "We wanted to communicate the up-to-date technology of the company while giving a corporate feel," says Desantos. The other colors, including black, gray, and white, were chosen to complement the blue. The color palette also appears in the Flash animation that moves across the top of the screen. By building a site around a corporate color, yet offering a lighter hue and a supporting color palette, uRreal combines the trust and professionalism of a corporate design with the innovative nature of their product for a solid blend of inventiveness and tradition.

When designing the site for Commerce One, an e-business solutions provider, Terry Green of twenty2product looked at corporate colors. Because the company had its roots in financial services, he knew he had to stay within a certain range of corporate design. A professional tone is critical when

COMMERCE ONE

ABOUT US   **BUYSITE**   MARKETSITE   CONTENT MANAGEMENT

NEWS & EVENTS   **PRODUCTS**   SERVICES   CUSTOMERS   SUPPLIERS   PARTNERS

BUYSITE
COMMERCE CHAIN SOLUTION

REQUISITION
Includes both
professional buyer
and end user

SELECTION
Includes both
professional buyer
and end user

APPROVAL
Includes both
professional buyer
and end user

dealing with large, traditional companies. The start of the color palette with tan colors came directly from the client. From there, Green built out the designs to reflect solid, safe dependability with a fresh touch. The blue highlight colors reinforce the blue of the logo and speak to the steadiness associated with the color.

On secondary pages, Green explored even more inventive uses of design with a traditionally corporate color palette. The visuals reinforce the professional, solid nature of the business. The images, including a chain evoking security, people in meetings and at work, along with the logo, convey the professionalism of the company and their services. By continuing the cool blue tones in a more muted manner, Green brought an innovative feel to the design while maintaining the sense of stability and professionalism critical to the company. Across other secondary pages, he continued the imagery. Building on the power of the chain, and the security it signifies, he added his range of slightly subdued, yet fresh tones, exploring tints of red against tints of green. The simplicity of the design, with its consistent messaging allows these designs to move beyond the traditional to the more evocative, while building on the imagery and branding of Commerce One.

1   173

27   65   9

28   40   173

173   38   30

5   173

1   163   79

38   163   39

60   164

40   168   37

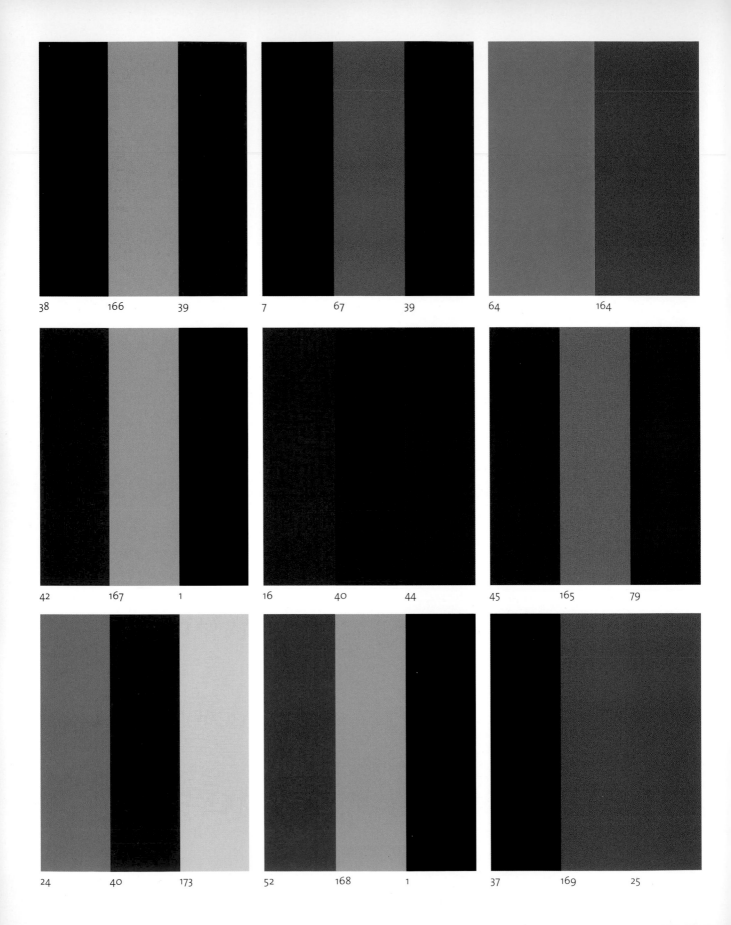

38   166   39

7   67   39

64   164

42   167   1

16   40   44

45   165   79

24   40   173

52   168   1

37   169   25

Throughout COLOR HARMONY FOR THE WEB several colors appear incorrectly. They should properly be printed as follows:

Color #48 (R51 G51 B255) should be printed as

Color #149 (R204 G0 B204) should be printed as

Color #199 (R255 G153 B0) should be printed as

Color #200 (R255 G153 B51) should be printed as

Color #201 (R255 G153 B102) should be printed as

Color #202 (R255 G153 B153) should be printed as

Color #203 (R255 G153 B204) should be printed as

Color #204 (R255 G153 B255) should be printed as

Color #210 (R255 G204 B255) should be printed as

Additionally:

Pages 175 & 178 Color #6 should be noted as R0 G0 B255 (not B225)
Page 178 Color #19 should be noted as R0 G153 B0 (not B00–this
does not affect accuracy)
Pages 176 & 186 Color #159 should be noted as R204 G102 B102 (not B153)

The Publisher apologizes for any confusion.

40   172   28

130   44   48

44   180   132

52   180   1

145   180   48

55   179   180

37   41   185

47   171   27

33   173

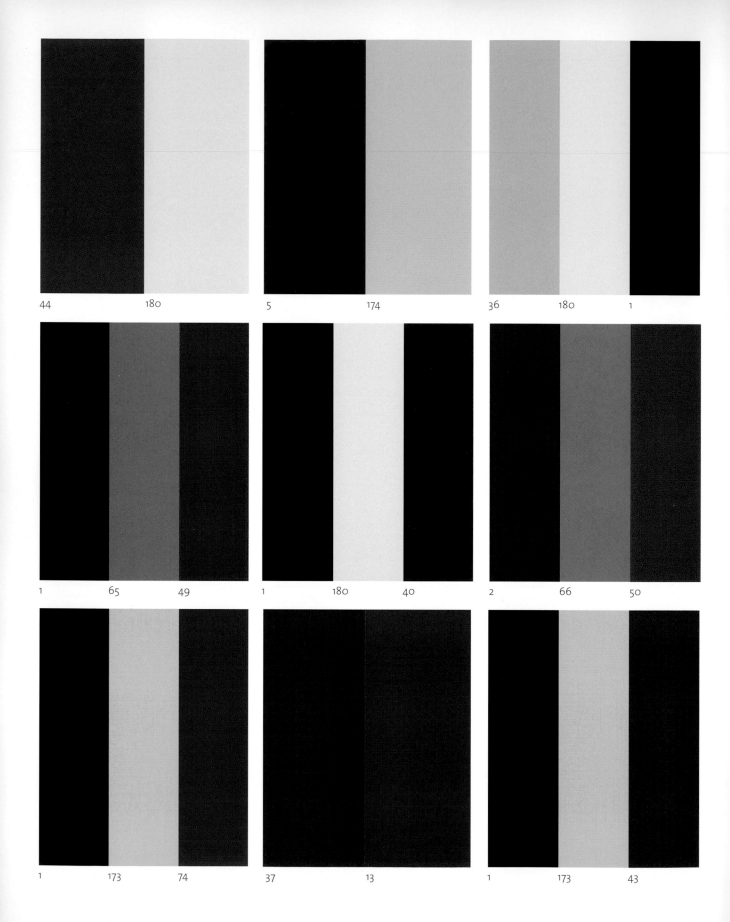

44   180   5   174   36   180   1

1   65   49   1   180   40   2   66   50

1   173   74   37   13   1   173   43

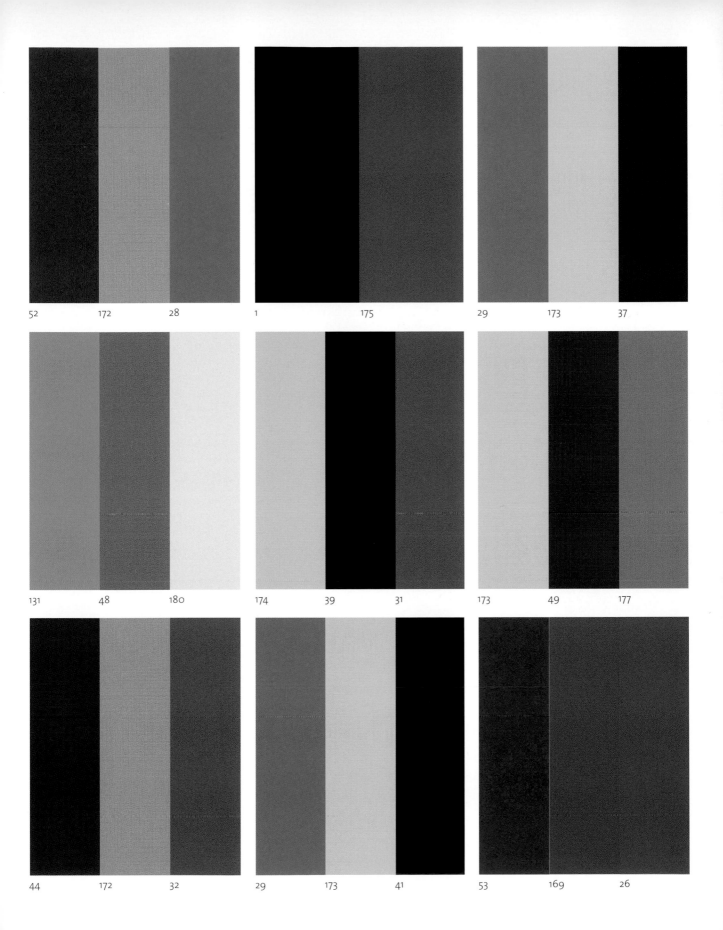

52	172	28
1	175	
29	173	37

131	48	180
174	39	31
173	49	177

44	172	32
29	173	41
53	169	26

Elegant

The PR Hub site was developed in 1999 by Darren Campeau, art director of Campeau Communications in San Francisco, for a range of software products targeted at the public relations industry. "We believe that the industry has a high concentration of women, so we wanted a site that reached them with a professional, elegant, and classic design," says Campeau. The softer images convey a warmth to the site that is distinctly not aggressive, making the site more appealing to women. The purple and orange of the identity offered an offbeat start to the color palette; the added brightness implies an inner light source. "We wanted a Mondrian feeling of color," says Campeau. The image on the right changes regularly for a fresh feel at every visit. The result is a nontraditional color palette that creates a sense of timelessness, continuity, and

dependability—powerful positioning for any product.

When looking for a mood for the Race for the Cure site, which promotes breast cancer awareness, the creative team at Webb Design in San Francisco knew exactly what they wanted: elegance. They began with a simple, graceful design and enhanced it with rich colors. The result is a deeply memorable site and refined color palette. "We wanted to avoid the typical pink and red colors usually associated with breast cancer," says Kim Webb, creative director. "We wanted a very different look and feel." The site is gentle and timeless in design. The images of the women are slightly blurred to convey the idea of every woman. The rich purple and blues express a classic elegance.

san francisco
RACE FOR THE CURE

Race for the Cure

menu ⬍

Komen Foundation

menu ⬍

Celebrate the 10th Anniversary Komen Race for the Cure in San Francisco on Sunday, October 1 2000.

Welcome to the Bay Area Affiliate of the Susan B. Komen Breast Cancer Foundation click the logo on top to return to this Welcom Page.

We are located in the Presidio of San Francisco.

Major Grants Applications Are Currently Being Accepted.

The Post Mark Deadline is Wednesday, May 3 2000. Applications are available on the Web for printing. Please click on the Community Grants on the left hand side of the Welcom Page.

Questions may be addressedt to grants@sfkomen.org

The San Francisco Bay Area Affiliate of the Susan G. Komen Breast Cancer Foundation

The GiftEmporia site created at 300 Feet Out, in San Francisco, allows visitors to shop at unique gift stores around the country. These independent shops carry special products, but rarely have an online presence. Visitors can create a gift registry from specialty shops across the country, or purchase a gift for faraway friends at shops they especially like. The target audience is upscale women, so it was critical that the site reflect the elegance of the stores. "We designed the site to capture the richness of choice available at GiftEmporia," says Kha Hoang, designer. The regal purple with silvery gray accent colors of the home page, which are continued through the secondary pages, bring a grace to the color palette. As visitors to the site click beyond the home page, they are greeted by clean, polished-looking pages and design. The quality of the gift items sold is so high that the design had to reflect the selection while providing a distinctive background against which to display the high-end, often one-of-a-kind products. The combination of elegant colors and exquisite design befits this portal to the finest gift stores in the country.

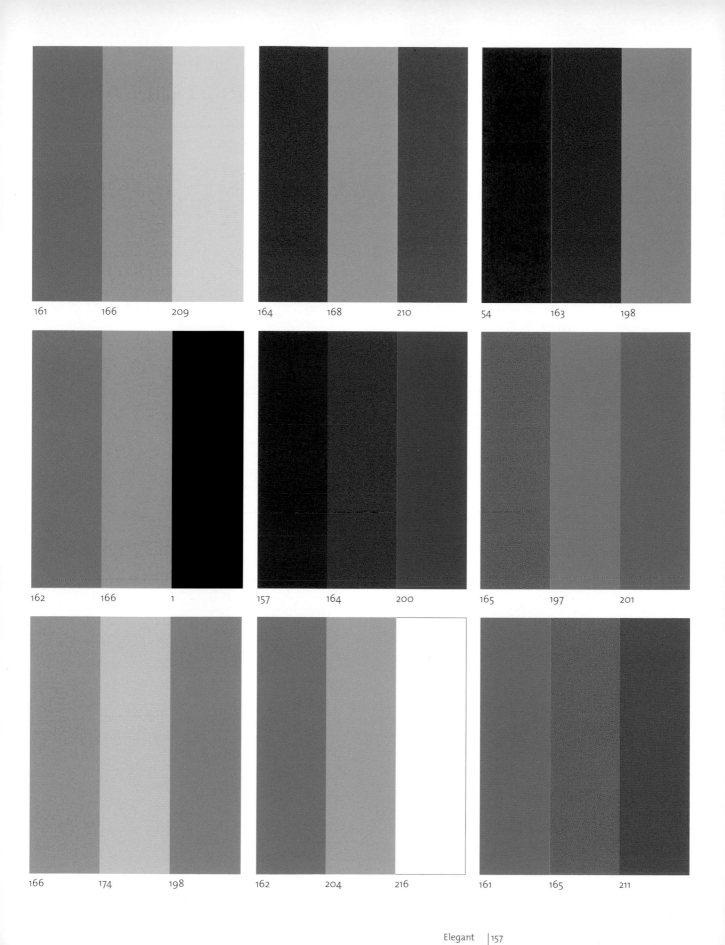

161   166   209

164   168   210

54   163   198

162   166   1

157   164   200

165   197   201

166   174   198

162   204   216

161   165   211

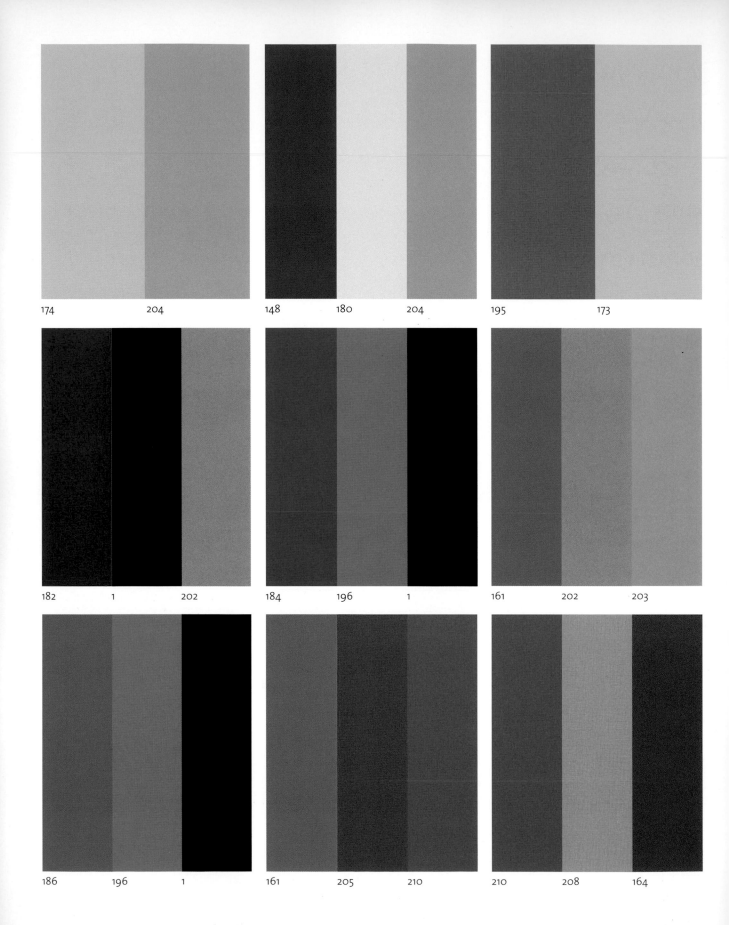

174   204

148   180   204

195   173

182   1   202

184   196   1

161   202   203

186   196   1

161   205   210

210   208   164

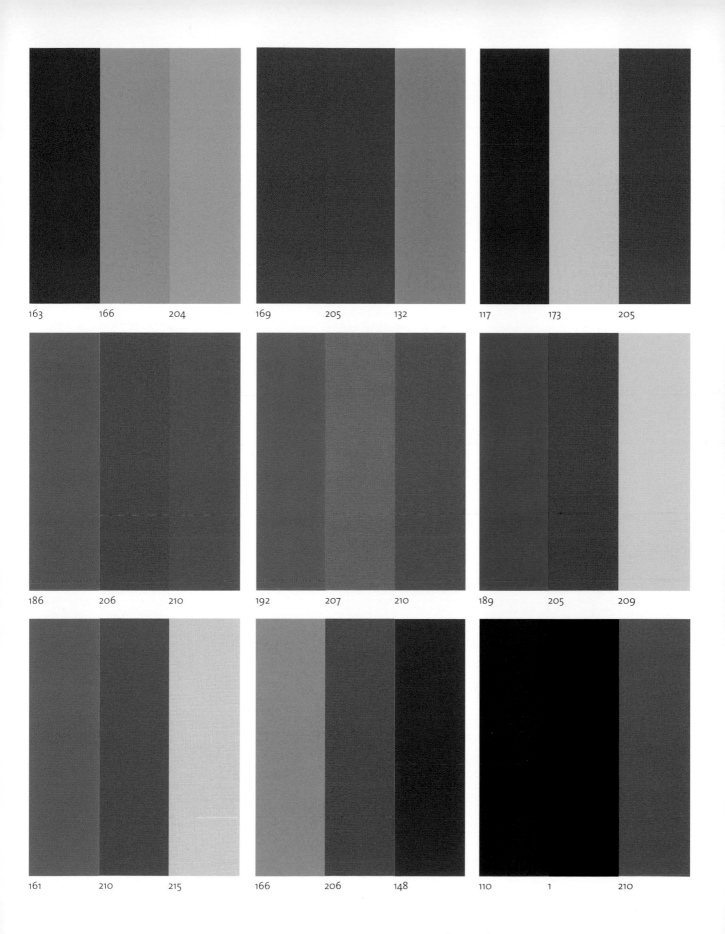

163   166   204   169   205   132   117   173   205

186   206   210   192   207   210   189   205   209

161   210   215   166   206   148   110   1   210

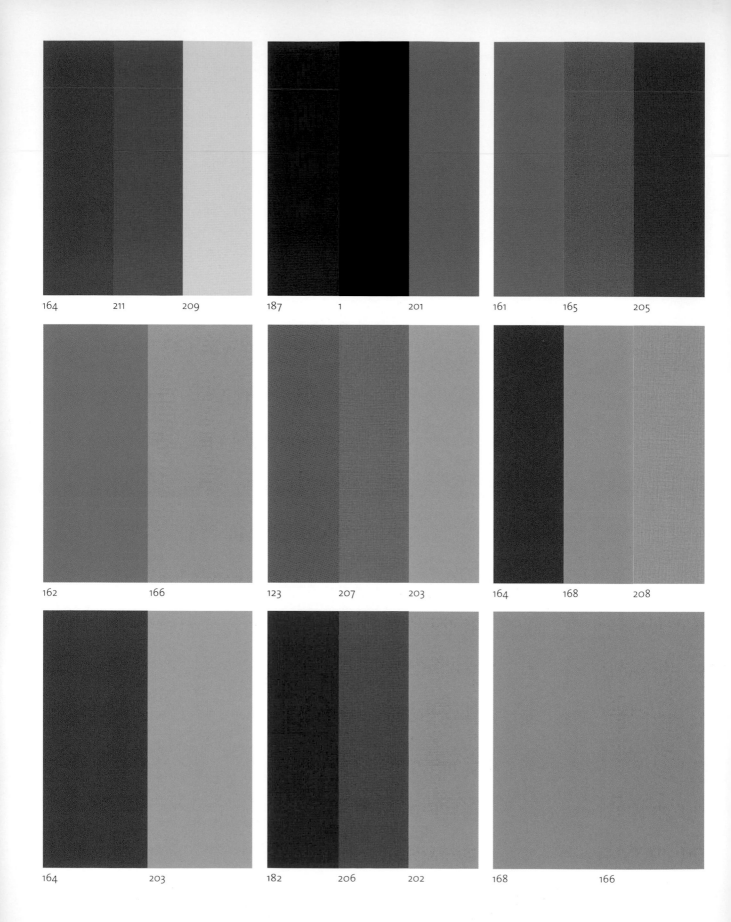

164   211   209   187   1   201   161   165   205

162   166   123   207   203   164   168   208

164   203   182   206   202   168   166

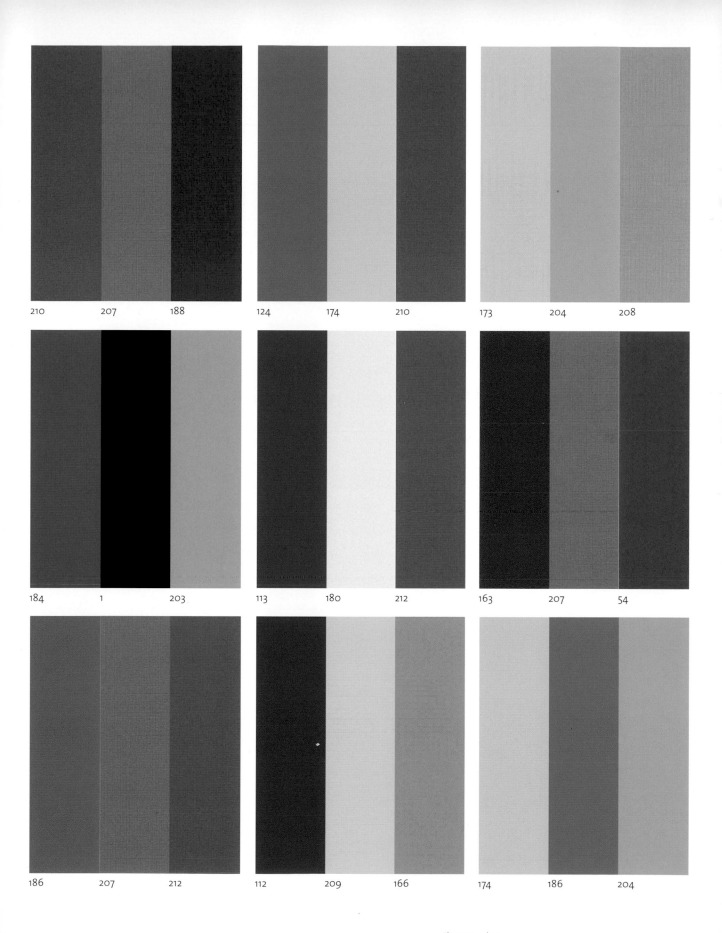

210   207   188   124   174   210   173   204   208

184   1   203   113   180   212   163   207   54

186   207   212   112   209   166   174   186   204

Welcoming

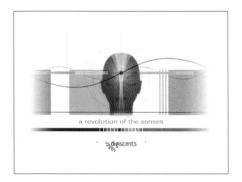

a revolution of the senses

digiscents

The DigiScents design, created by Terry Green at twenty2product, has a soothing, welcoming color palette. "The challenge of DigiScents, a fragrance company," says Green, "is to evoke the feeling of a scent through a medium that doesn't allow smell." With this objective, the choice of colors was critical. Muted tones create a peaceful feeling; the breadth of the palette matches the range of the fragrances available. By using color to communicate scent, Green created an inviting, accessible design that matches the tone of DigiScents itself.

The Hawaii International Film Fest site was designed in 1999 for the annual celebration of motion pictures in Honolulu. The festival features movies from around the world, with an emphasis on Asia and the Pacific. "If you're tired of watching Hollywood clichés and unnecessary explosions on screen, then the HIFF won't disappoint you," says Steven Tu, designer at RevaComm in Honolulu. "Many of the movies are produced on small budgets and reveal the diversity of cultures, especially in Asia, and human conditions from perspectives other than that of Hollywood." The black and white photography overlying the vivid background, the strong typography, and electrifying colors capture the experimental spirit of the young filmmakers. The soft blue and bright yellow highlights evoke Hawaii's sun and sea. Complementary colors give a sense of harmony and structure. Above all, the colors produce a welcoming feel that accurately portrays HIFF as an approachable, inclusive event.

HAWAII INTERNATIONAL
FILM FESTIVAL

1999

1999 FILM FESTIVAL MOVIE LISTING

GENERAL INFORMATION

ORDER TICKETS

JOIN FILM FANS

CALL FOR ENTRIES

CONTACT INFORMATION

OUR HEROES

CULTURAL & VISUAL LITERACY PROGRAM

FILM DISCUSSION GROUP

FILM ARCHIVE

The Chefwear site is a market for people in the restaurant industry. Chefwear offers a full range of culinary apparel, from hats and aprons to uniquely designed pants. Creating the site in the fall of 1999, the team at DNA Visual Business Solutions in Chicago began with the company's corporate catalog. The bright color palette was offset with a black background so the product images could take over the screen. "We wanted the site to be clean, simple and fun," says Karen Shields, creative director. Aimed at professional and at-home cooks, the site had to welcome both groups. The bright colors create a visually rich site that appeals to the range of people shopping for foodservice clothing. Starting with bright colors, the site celebrates its products. Vivid colors, from cooler blues to purples and fresh greens up to yellows and reds, jump out from the site's black horizontal frame. The animated feeling makes the site and its products accessible. This visual tone continues on the other pages, where colors jump off the screen. By blending a sense of fun in the drawings with a bright, welcoming palette, this design evokes a welcoming feel to the range of cooks, whether professional or amateur, who come to the site.

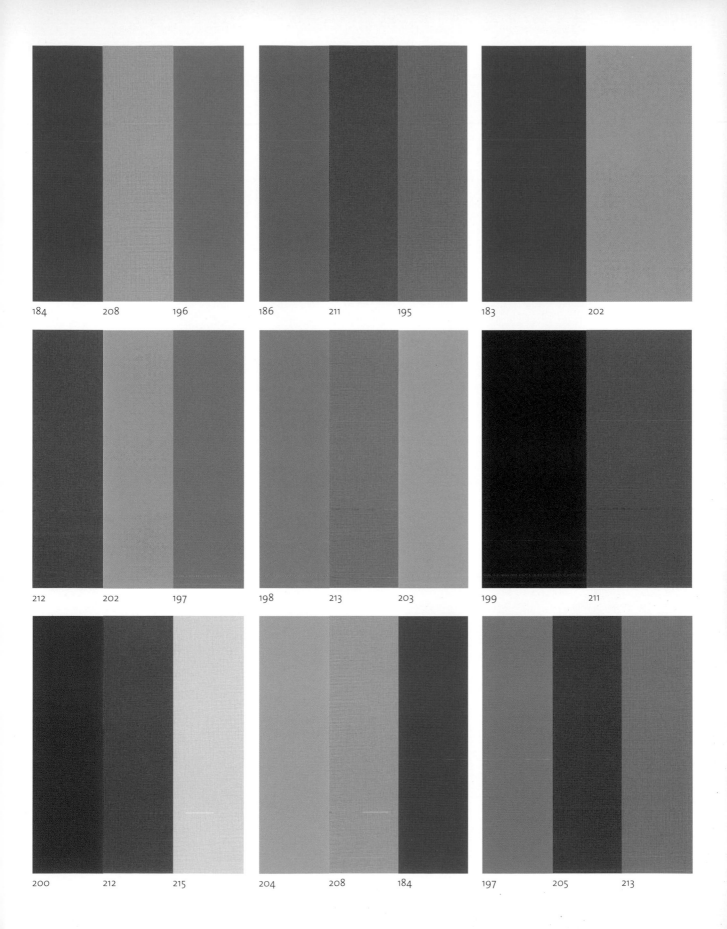

184   208   196   186   211   195   183   202

212   202   197   198   213   203   199   211

200   212   215   204   208   184   197   205   213

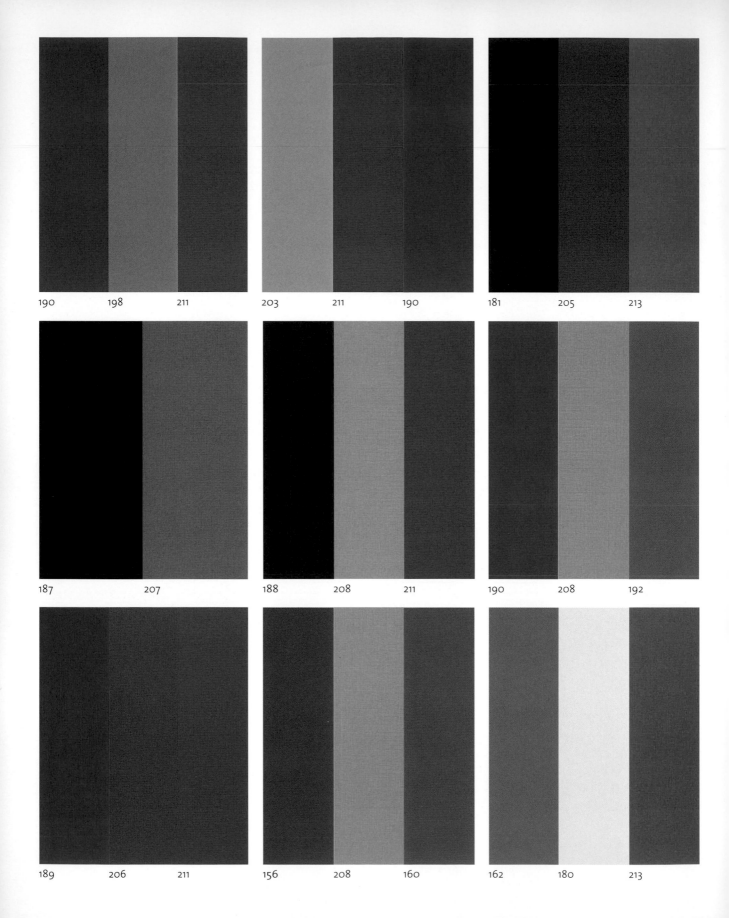

190   198   211

203   211   190

181   205   213

187   207

188   208   211

190   208   192

189   206   211

156   208   160

162   180   213

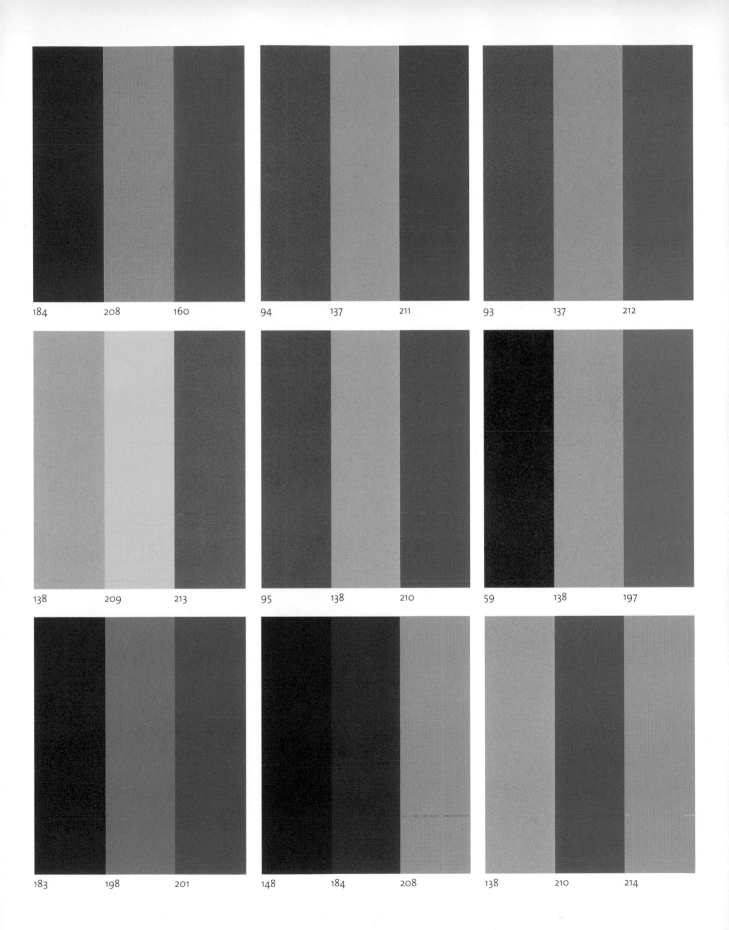

184 208 160

94 137 211

93 137 212

138 209 213

95 138 210

59 138 197

183 198 201

148 184 208

138 210 214

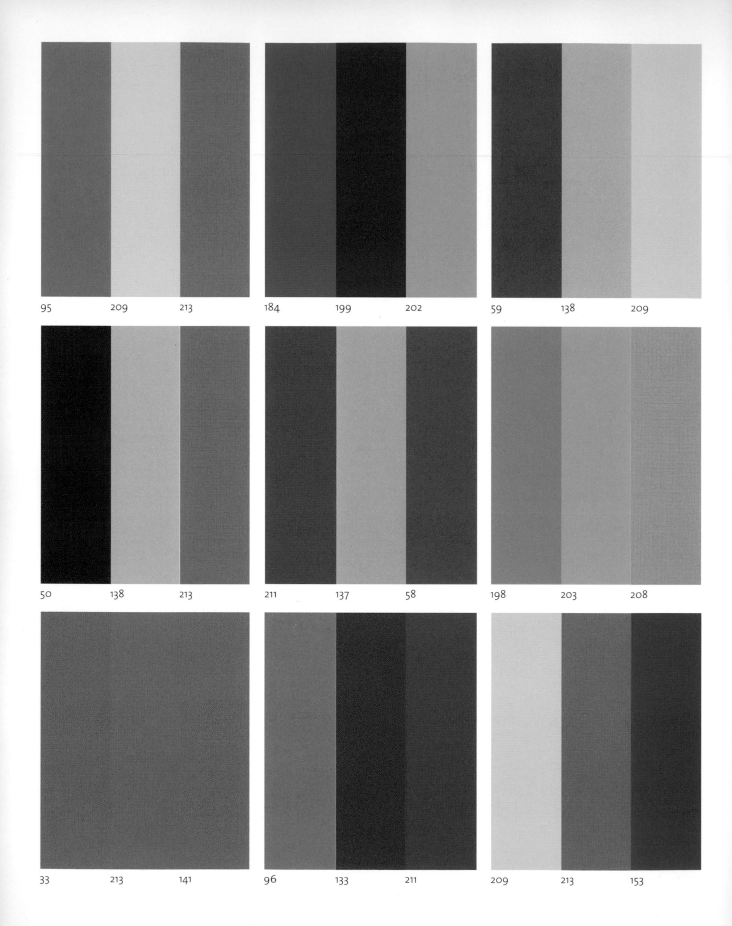

95	209	213
184	199	202
59	138	209

50	138	213
211	137	58
198	203	208

33	213	141
96	133	211
209	213	153

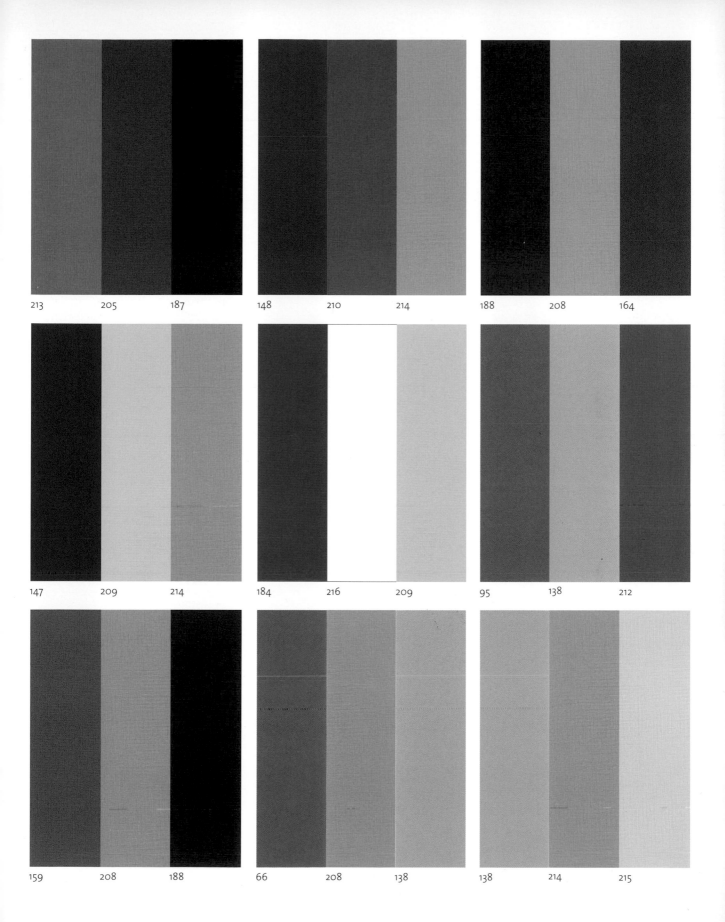

213   205   187   148   210   214   188   208   164

147   209   214   184   216   209   95   138   212

159   208   188   66   208   138   138   214   215

Going Forward

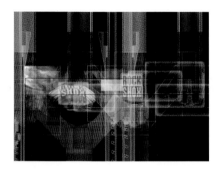

Trying to predict where the web is going is like trying to catch mercury; pressure in one area results in movement in another, and you never know where it's going to go—only where it's been.

With that caveat in mind, we spoke with people at the forefront of web design and asked them what they see in the future of the web.

Color and Design

Color was the first dimension most often mentioned. Currently, most designers try to create sites by staying within the web-safe color palette. However, this convention is fading away. The restriction is based on the limitations of monitors. With each passing month, a greater percentage of monitors are able to show all colors. Currently, about 84 percent of monitors can use all colors, and this number will only increase as old computers are replaced and new ones become the standard. We'll see even more vibrant use of color as designers feel freer to use the entire range of the spectrum.

Stephen Bishop sees the change in the availability of color as an opportunity and a challenge. "With advancements in technology, the number of colors able to be accurately presented on screen will expand from the current 216 to millions. Resolution will follow the same path. Achieving color harmony on the web will take the same level of skill and precision currently required in print design. And doing so will be critical to the success or failure of the web designer's work."

cocktail →

Says Nina Dietzel, "I think people are becoming more sophisticated and therefore are willing to take more risks, especially when it comes to color. As well, a lot of the more sophisticated sensibilities from print, such as smaller type, more use of white space, and more imagery are interestingly applied to the web."

Bandwidth

Flash animation and moving images are quickly capturing the imagination of users. Some sites have static images, as the creators don't want viewers to wait

for a long download. However, as bandwidth becomes less of a constraint and more people move from dial-up modems to DSL, file size limitations, like color limitations, will expand. Says Land Good, "Life is full of color and motion. More and more, the web too will be filled with movement and beauty. Flash and QuickTime movies will certainly play a large part in the web's future."

Terry Green agrees. "What's been the most surprising thing for me is the motion graphics work that's being done for web sites in Flash, in many ways lots more impressive than anything I've seen done specifically for broadcast, and with much more affordable equipment. I think it's safe to assume that motion graphics will grow to be an even bigger part of how products and services are communicated. The simultaneous work of international design talent will continue to expand ideas of what constitutes acceptable design. Equipment and fast Internet connections will become less expensive and therefore more accessible. Overall, I think the web is a great inspiration for design."

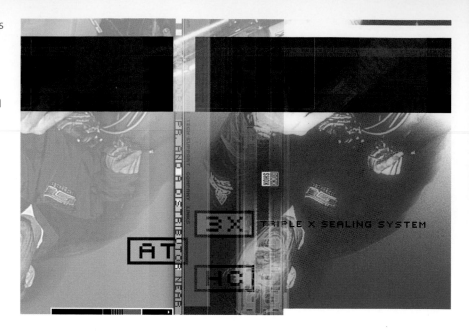

John Caserta sees the limitations decreasing. "Narrowband will continue to improve until it becomes broadband, and bandwidth, scripting, and monitor limitations diminish annually. Today's designs that still limit themselves to a page metaphor can become more liberated and use more interface-like elements to communicate even more effectively to users. The challenge is to not let the masses drive all designs into the same look and feel. Sites, like books, should each have a different quality. And that differentiation helps them succeed."

Stephen Bishop says, "Designers will evolve with the web as it becomes a medium for entertainment. Hardware will evolve, bandwidth will broaden, and software will bring more and more dimensions to web design. Flash and streaming technologies are already adding motion to what was once a static discipline. Animation is spreading across the web and broadcast video is not far behind. The future web designer will resemble one of three things: a film director, a cinematographer, or a set designer. The designer's skill sets must adapt accordingly."

International Considerations

Gena Uehara says, "Web designers are information architects, ontologists, as well as communication designers. Because the Internet is an interactive medium, designers need to know how to construct information according to its level of importance and ease of use while keeping the client's brand and target audience in mind at all times. As ontologists, designers need to think about how a user reads a page and try to keep the user engaged at all times by making the navigational experience simple, easy, and pain-free. For example, words, images, and color selected for an American audience will differ for a Japanese audience because the cultures and reading processes are different. Thus, designers need to be culturally in tune with and sensitive to this diversity, which will affect a web site's content and layout structure."

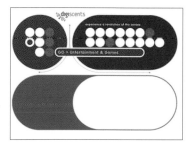

Branding

Nina Dietzel believes that branding will be one of the strongest drivers in web design in the future.

"I think there is a fringe movement right now that is reexamining what branding stands for today. The web is so immediate and needs to be satisfying for an increasing number of people with decreasing available time. While it's important to break through all the clutter of visual pollution, at the same time we must come up with fresh ideas and different takes on what the standards of branding should be. This is the time to reinvent the standards of the industry on many levels.

As much as branding needs to be consistent, it needs to be alive and not become too static. At 300 Feet Out, we try to develop systems that are a little more free-form. We're questioning constantly the level of branding that a company or group of people really needs. To me, in the pre-web days, it was much more a question of 'What do we want to stand for?' on a very outward level, versus now it's 'Who are we? What do we do?' It's much more internal, much more immediate. It's about capturing the feeling of a group of people who walk into the room with a new business plan under their arm. It's how they dress, where they choose to have their offices, what energy they support in their work world, how driven they are, and how all the above is translated into their specific visual language."

Content

Stephen Bishop sees the growth of content as the greatest challenge. "Web designers are faced with a future that depends more and more on information. The amount of data generated continues to grow, and web designers will do more to shape it into information that can easily be understood. This will lead to new ways of seeing and presenting over the web. It must. Creating new ways of seeing is the greatest challenge in the future of web design. It is also the greatest opportunity."

It's a Wireless World

As the web expands, so does the demand for wireless technology. The expansion of hand-held devices and web-capable cell phones means that design for the web is no longer limited to computer-based viewing. The new focus will be on how to create a unified, branded experience across all devices.

Gena Uehara highlights the importance of the fundamentals in the future. "In collaboration with marketers, designers will still need to focus on communicating a message by following the historical rule *form follows function*.

Function is the message for a specific audience. Form is the way the message is communicated to that audience. It is through a combination of information design, aesthetics, and user market data that effective designers will continue to create for both print and new media. With the advent of wireless and personal technology, this messaging challenge will grow. Designers will need to take into consideration the variety of wireless application standards, operating systems, browser sizes, colors, and load time when creating design."

Concludes Tim Barber, "Web design for the PC is being transformed by new devices and communications mechanisms as well as advances in PC performance. Brands that will survive and succeed in the future will reach out to audiences with compelling and appropriate experiences on each of the devices their customers use—mobile Internet appliances, interactive TVs, and broadband PCs. These experiences will have to use a broader toolkit to achieve their objectives. Color, typography, interactivity, motion, functionality, etc., will be essential to this new, expanded branding toolkit."

Color Conversion Chart

COLOR	NUMBER	R	G	B	HEX #	COLOR	NUMBER	R	G	B	HEX #
	1	0	0	0	#000000		55	51	153	0	#339900
	2	0	0	51	#000033		56	51	153	51	#339933
	3	0	0	102	#000066		57	51	153	102	#339966
	4	0	0	153	#000099		58	51	153	153	#339999
	5	0	0	204	#0000CC		59	51	153	204	#3399CC
	6	0	0	225	#0000FF		60	51	153	255	#3399FF
	7	0	51	0	#003300		61	51	204	0	#33CC00
	8	0	51	51	#003333		62	51	204	51	#33CC33
	9	0	51	102	#003366		63	51	204	102	#33CC66
	10	0	51	153	#003399		64	51	204	153	#33CC99
	11	0	51	204	#0033CC		65	51	204	204	#33CCCC
	12	0	51	255	#0033FF		66	51	204	255	#33CCFF
	13	0	102	0	#006600		67	51	255	0	#33FF00
	14	0	102	51	#006633		68	51	255	51	#33FF33
	15	0	102	102	#006666		69	51	255	102	#33FF66
	16	0	102	153	#006699		70	51	255	153	#33FF99
	17	0	102	204	#0066CC		71	51	255	204	#33FFCC
	18	0	102	255	#0066FF		72	51	255	255	#33FFFF
	19	0	153	00	#009900		73	102	0	0	#660000
	20	0	153	51	#009933		74	102	0	51	#660033
	21	0	153	102	#009966		75	102	0	102	#660066
	22	0	153	153	#009999		76	102	0	153	#660099
	23	0	153	204	#0099CC		77	102	0	204	#6600CC
	24	0	153	255	#0099FF		78	102	0	255	#6600FF
	25	0	204	0	#00CC00		79	102	51	0	#663300
	26	0	204	51	#00CC33		80	102	51	51	#663333
	27	0	204	102	#00CC66		81	102	51	102	#663366
	28	0	204	153	#00CC99		82	102	51	153	#663399
	29	0	204	204	#00CCCC		83	102	51	204	#6633CC
	30	0	204	255	#00CCFF		84	102	51	255	#6633FF
	31	0	255	0	#00FF00		85	102	102	0	#666600
	32	0	255	51	#00FF33		86	102	102	51	#666633
	33	0	255	102	#00FF66		87	102	102	102	#666666
	34	0	255	153	#00FF99		88	102	102	153	#666699
	35	0	255	204	#00FFCC		89	102	102	204	#6666CC
	36	0	255	255	#00FFFF		90	102	102	255	#6666FF
	37	51	0	0	#330000		91	102	153	0	#669900
	38	51	0	51	#330033		92	102	153	51	#669933
	39	51	0	102	#330066		93	102	153	102	#669966
	40	51	0	153	#330099		94	102	153	153	#669999
	41	51	0	204	#3300CC		95	102	153	204	#6699CC
	42	51	0	255	#3300FF		96	102	153	255	#6699FF
	43	51	51	0	#333300		97	102	204	0	#66CC00
	44	51	51	51	#333333		98	102	204	51	#66CC33
	45	51	51	102	#333366		99	102	204	102	#66CC66
	46	51	51	153	#333399		100	102	204	153	#66CC99
	47	51	51	204	#3333CC		101	102	204	204	#66CCCC
	48	51	51	255	#3333FF		102	102	204	255	#66CCFF
	49	51	102	0	#336600		103	102	255	0	#66FF00
	50	51	102	51	#336633		104	102	255	51	#66FF33
	51	51	102	102	#336666		105	102	255	102	#66FF66
	52	51	102	153	#336699		106	102	255	153	#66FF99
	53	51	102	204	#3366CC		107	102	255	204	#66FFCC
	54	51	102	255	#3366FF		108	102	255	255	#66FFFF

Color Conversion Chart

COLOR NUMBER	R	G	B	HEX #	COLOR NUMBER	R	G	B	HEX #
109	153	0	0	#990000	163	204	153	0	#CC9900
110	153	0	51	#990033	164	204	153	51	#CC9933
111	153	0	102	#990066	165	204	153	102	#CC9966
112	153	0	153	#990099	166	204	153	153	#CC9999
113	153	0	204	#9900CC	167	204	153	204	#CC99CC
114	153	0	255	#9900FF	168	204	153	255	#CC99FF
115	153	51	0	#993300	169	204	204	0	#CCCCo
116	153	51	51	#993333	170	204	204	51	#CCCC33
117	153	51	102	#993366	171	204	204	102	#CCCC66
118	153	51	153	#993399	172	204	204	153	#CCCC99
119	153	51	204	#9933CC	173	204	204	204	#CCCCCC
120	153	51	255	#9933FF	174	204	204	255	#CCCCFF
121	153	102	0	#996600	175	204	255	0	#CCFFoo
122	153	102	51	#996633	176	204	255	51	#CCFF33
123	153	102	102	#996666	177	204	255	102	#CCFF66
124	153	102	153	#996699	178	204	255	153	#CCFF99
125	153	102	204	#9966CC	179	204	255	204	#CCFFCC
126	153	102	255	#9966FF	180	204	255	255	#CCFFFF
127	153	153	0	#999900	181	255	0	0	#FFoooo
128	153	153	51	#999933	182	255	0	51	#FFoo33
129	153	153	102	#999966	183	255	0	102	#FFoo66
130	153	153	153	#999999	184	255	0	153	#FFoo99
131	153	153	204	#9999CC	185	255	0	204	#FFooCC
132	153	153	255	#9999FF	186	255	0	255	#FFooFF
133	153	204	0	#99CCoo	187	255	51	0	#FF3300
134	153	204	51	#99CC33	188	255	51	51	#FF3333
135	153	204	102	#99CC66	189	255	51	102	#FF3366
136	153	204	153	#99CC99	190	255	51	153	#FF3399
137	153	204	204	#99CCCC	191	255	51	204	#FF33CC
138	153	204	255	#99CCFF	192	255	51	255	#FF33FF
139	153	255	0	#99FFoo	193	255	102	0	#FF6600
140	153	255	51	#99FF33	194	255	102	51	#FF6633
141	153	255	102	#99FF66	195	255	102	102	#FF6666
142	153	255	153	#99FF99	196	255	102	153	#FF6699
143	153	255	204	#99FFCC	197	255	102	204	#FF66CC
144	153	255	255	#99FFFF	198	255	102	255	#FF66FF
145	204	0	0	#CCoooo	199	255	153	0	#FF9900
146	204	0	51	#CCoo33	200	255	153	51	#FF9933
147	204	0	102	#CCoo66	201	255	153	102	#FF9966
148	204	0	153	#CCoo99	202	255	153	153	#FF9999
149	204	0	204	#CCooCC	203	255	153	204	#FF99CC
150	204	0	255	#CCooFF	204	255	153	255	#FF99FF
151	204	51	0	#CC3300	205	255	204	0	#FFCCoo
152	204	51	51	#CC3333	206	255	204	51	#FFCC33
153	204	51	102	#CC3366	207	255	204	102	#FFCC66
154	204	51	153	#CC3399	208	255	204	153	#FFCC99
155	204	51	204	#CC33CC	209	255	204	204	#FFCCCC
156	204	51	255	#CC33FF	210	255	204	255	#FFCCFF
157	204	102	0	#CC6600	211	255	255	0	#FFFFoo
158	204	102	51	#CC6633	212	255	255	51	#FFFF33
159	204	102	153	#CC6666	213	255	255	102	#FFFF66
160	204	102	153	#CC6699	214	255	255	153	#FFFF99
161	204	102	204	#CC66CC	215	255	255	204	#FFFFCC
162	204	102	255	#CC66FF	216	255	255	255	#FFFFFF

6		**5**		**4**		**3**		**2**		**1**	
R 0		**R** 0		**R** 0		**R** 0		**R** 0		**R** 0	
G 0		**G** 0		**G** 0		**G** 0		**G** 0		**G** 0	
B 225		**B** 204		**B** 153		**B** 102		**B** 51		**B** 0	
# 0000FF		# 0000CC		# 000099		# 000066		# 000033		# 000000	

12		**11**		**10**		**9**		**8**		**7**	
R 0		**R** 0		**R** 0		**R** 0		**R** 0		**R** 0	
G 51		**G** 51		**G** 51		**G** 51		**G** 51		**G** 51	
B 255		**B** 204		**B** 153		**B** 102		**B** 51		**B** 0	
# 0033FF		# 0033CC		# 003399		# 003366		# 003333		# 003300	

18		**17**		**16**		**15**		**14**		**13**	
R 0		**R** 0		**R** 0		**R** 0		**R** 0		**R** 0	
G 102		**G** 102		**G** 102		**G** 102		**G** 102		**G** 102	
B 255		**B** 204		**B** 153		**B** 102		**B** 51		**B** 0	
# 0066FF		# 0066CC		# 006699		# 006666		# 006633		# 006600	

24		**23**		**22**		**21**		**20**		**19**	
R 0		**R** 0		**R** 0		**R** 0		**R** 0		**R** 0	
G 153		**G** 153		**G** 153		**G** 153		**G** 153		**G** 153	
B 255		**B** 204		**B** 153		**B** 102		**B** 51		**B** 00	
# 0099FF		# 0099CC		# 009999		# 009966		# 009933		# 009900	

30		**29**		**28**		**27**		**26**		**25**	
R 0		**R** 0		**R** 0		**R** 0		**R** 0		**R** 0	
G 204		**G** 204		**G** 204		**G** 204		**G** 204		**G** 204	
B 255		**B** 204		**B** 153		**B** 102		**B** 51		**B** 0	
# 00CCFF		# 00CCCC		# 00CC99		# 00CC66		# 00CC33		# 00CC00	

36		**35**		**34**		**33**		**32**		**31**	
R 0		**R** 0		**R** 0		**R** 0		**R** 0		**R** 0	
G 255		**G** 255		**G** 255		**G** 255		**G** 255		**G** 255	
B 255		**B** 204		**B** 153		**B** 102		**B** 51		**B** 0	
# 00FFFF		# 00FFCC		# 00FF99		# 00FF66		# 00FF33		# 00FF00	

42	**41**	**40**	**39**	**38**	**37**
R 51	R 51	R 51	R 51	R 51	R 51
G 0	G 0	G 0	G 0	G 0	G 0
B 255	B 204	B 153	B 102	B 51	B 0
# 3300FF	# 3300CC	# 330099	# 330066	# 330033	# 330000

48	**47**	**46**	**45**	**44**	**43**
R 51	R 51	R 51	R 51	R 51	R 51
G 51	G 51	G 51	G 51	G 51	G 51
B 255	B 204	B 153	B 102	B 51	B 0
# 3333FF	# 3333CC	# 333399	# 333366	# 333333	# 333300

54	**53**	**52**	**51**	**50**	**49**
R 51	R 51	R 51	R 51	R 51	R 51
G 102	G 102	G 102	G 102	G 102	G 102
B 255	B 204	B 153	B 102	B 51	B 0
# 3366FF	# 3366CC	# 336699	# 336666	# 336633	# 336600

60	**59**	**58**	**57**	**56**	**55**
R 51	R 51	R 51	R 51	R 51	R 51
G 153	G 153	G 153	G 153	G 153	G 153
B 255	B 204	B 153	B 102	B 51	B 0
# 3399FF	# 3399CC	# 339999	# 339966	# 339933	# 339900

66	**65**	**64**	**63**	**62**	**61**
R 51	R 51	R 51	R 51	R 51	R 51
G 204	G 204	G 204	G 204	G 204	G 204
B 255	B 204	B 153	B 102	B 51	B 0
# 33CCFF	# 33CCCC	# 33CC99	# 33CC66	# 33CC33	# 33CC00

72	**71**	**70**	**69**	**68**	**67**
R 51	R 51	R 51	R 51	R 51	R 51
G 255	G 255	G 255	G 255	G 255	G 255
B 255	B 204	B 153	B 102	B 51	B 0
# 33FFFF	# 33FFCC	# 33FF99	# 33FF66	# 33FF33	# 33FF00

78 R 102 G 0 B 255 # 6600FF	**77** R 102 G 0 B 204 # 6600CC	**76** R 102 G 0 B 153 # 660099	**75** R 102 G 0 B 102 # 660066	**74** R 102 G 0 B 51 # 660033	**73** R 102 G 0 B 0 # 660000
84 R 102 G 51 B 255 # 6633FF	**83** R 102 G 51 B 204 # 6633CC	**82** R 102 G 51 B 153 # 663399	**81** R 102 G 51 B 102 # 663366	**80** R 102 G 51 B 51 # 663333	**79** R 102 G 51 B 0 # 663300
90 R 102 G 102 B 255 # 6666FF	**89** R 102 G 102 B 204 # 6666CC	**88** R 102 G 102 B 153 # 666699	**87** R 102 G 102 B 102 # 666666	**86** R 102 G 102 B 51 # 666633	**85** R 102 G 102 B 0 # 666600
96 R 102 G 153 B 255 # 6699FF	**95** R 102 G 153 B 204 # 6699CC	**94** R 102 G 153 B 153 # 669999	**93** R 102 G 153 B 102 # 669966	**92** R 102 G 153 B 51 # 669933	**91** R 102 G 153 B 0 # 669900
102 R 102 G 204 B 255 # 66CCFF	**101** R 102 G 204 B 204 # 66CCCC	**100** R 102 G 204 B 153 # 66CC99	**99** R 102 G 204 B 102 # 66CC66	**98** R 102 G 204 B 51 # 66CC33	**97** R 102 G 204 B 0 # 66CC00
108 R 102 G 255 B 255 # 66FFFF	**107** R 102 G 255 B 204 # 66FFCC	**106** R 102 G 255 B 153 # 66FF99	**105** R 102 G 255 B 102 # 66FF66	**104** R 102 G 255 B 51 # 66FF33	**103** R 102 G 255 B 0 # 66FF00

114
R 153
G 0
B 255
9900FF

113
R 153
G 0
B 204
9900CC

112
R 153
G 0
B 153
990099

111
R 153
G 0
B 102
990066

110
R 153
G 0
B 51
990033

109
R 153
G 0
B 0
990000

120
R 153
G 51
B 255
9933FF

119
R 153
G 51
B 204
9933CC

118
R 153
G 51
B 153
993399

117
R 153
G 51
B 102
993366

116
R 153
G 51
B 51
993333

115
R 153
G 51
B 0
993300

126
R 153
G 102
B 255
9966FF

125
R 153
G 102
B 204
9966CC

124
R 153
G 102
B 153
996699

123
R 153
G 102
B 102
996666

122
R 153
G 102
B 51
996633

121
R 153
G 102
B 0
996600

132
R 153
G 153
B 255
9999FF

131
R 153
G 153
B 204
9999CC

130
R 153
G 153
B 153
999999

129
R 153
G 153
B 102
999966

128
R 153
G 153
B 51
999933

127
R 153
G 153
B 0
999900

138
R 153
G 204
B 255
99CCFF

137
R 153
G 204
B 204
99CCCC

136
R 153
G 204
B 153
99CC99

135
R 153
G 204
B 102
99CC66

134
R 153
G 204
B 51
99CC33

133
R 153
G 204
B 0
99CC00

144
R 153
G 255
B 255
99FFFF

143
R 153
G 255
B 204
99FFCC

142
R 153
G 255
B 153
99FF99

141
R 153
G 255
B 102
99FF66

140
R 153
G 255
B 51
99FF33

139
R 153
G 255
B 0
99FF00

150	**149**	**148**	**147**	**146**	**145**
R 204	R 204	R 204	R 204	R 204	R 204
G 0	G 0	G 0	G 0	G 0	G 0
B 255	B 204	B 153	B 102	B 51	B 0
# CC00FF	# CC00CC	# CC0099	# CC0066	# CC0033	# CC0000

156	**155**	**154**	**153**	**152**	**151**
R 204	R 204	R 204	R 204	R 204	R 204
G 51	G 51	G 51	G 51	G 51	G 51
B 255	B 204	B 153	B 102	B 51	B 0
# CC33FF	# CC33CC	# CC3399	# CC3366	# CC3333	# CC3300

162	**161**	**160**	**159**	**158**	**157**
R 204	R 204	R 204	R 204	R 204	R 204
G 102	G 102	G 102	G 102	G 102	G 102
B 255	B 204	B 153	B 153	B 51	B 0
# CC66FF	# CC66CC	# CC6699	# CC6666	# CC6633	# CC6600

168	**167**	**166**	**165**	**164**	**163**
R 204	R 204	R 204	R 204	R 204	R 204
G 153	G 153	G 153	G 153	G 153	G 153
B 255	B 204	B 153	B 102	B 51	B 0
# CC99FF	# CC99CC	# CC9999	# CC9966	# CC9933	# CC9900

174	**173**	**172**	**171**	**170**	**169**
R 204	R 204	R 204	R 204	R 204	R 204
G 204	G 204	G 204	G 204	G 204	G 204
B 255	B 204	B 153	B 102	B 51	B 0
# CCCCFF	# CCCCCC	# CCCC99	# CCCC66	# CCCC33	# CCCC0

180	**179**	**178**	**177**	**176**	**175**
R 204	R 204	R 178	R 204	R 204	R 204
G 255	G 255	G 204	G 255	G 255	G 255
B 255	B 204	B 255	B 102	B 51	B 0
# CCFFFF	# CCFFCC	#CCFF99	# CCFF66	# CCFF33	# CCFF00

186		**185**		**184**		**183**		**182**		**181**	
R 255		**R** 255		**R** 255		**R** 255		**R** 255		**R** 255	
G 0		**G** 0		**G** 0		**G** 0		**G** 0		**G** 0	
B 255		**B** 204		**B** 153		**B** 102		**B** 51		**B** 0	
# FF00FF		**#** FF00CC		**#** FF0099		**#** FF0066		**#** FF0033		**#** FF0000	

192		**191**		**190**		**189**		**188**		**187**	
R 255		**R** 255		**R** 255		**R** 255		**R** 255		**R** 255	
G 51		**G** 51		**G** 51		**G** 51		**G** 51		**G** 51	
B 255		**B** 204		**B** 153		**B** 102		**B** 51		**B** 0	
# FF33FF		**#** FF33CC		**#** FF3399		**#** FF3366		**#** FF3333		**#** FF3300	

198		**197**		**196**		**195**		**194**		**193**	
R 255		**R** 255		**R** 255		**R** 255		**R** 255		**R** 255	
G 102		**G** 102		**G** 102		**G** 102		**G** 102		**G** 102	
B 255		**B** 204		**B** 153		**B** 102		**B** 51		**B** 0	
# FF66FF		**#** FF66CC		**#** FF6699		**#** FF6666		**#** FF6633		**#** FF6600	

204		**203**		**202**		**201**		**200**		**199**	
R 255		**R** 255		**R** 255		**R** 255		**R** 255		**R** 255	
G 153		**G** 153		**G** 153		**G** 153		**G** 153		**G** 153	
B 255		**B** 204		**B** 153		**B** 102		**B** 51		**B** 0	
# FF99FF		**#** FF99CC		**#** FF9999		**#** FF9966		**#** FF9933		**#** FF9900	

210		**209**		**208**		**207**		**206**		**205**	
R 255		**R** 255		**R** 255		**R** 255		**R** 255		**R** 255	
G 204		**G** 204		**G** 204		**G** 204		**G** 204		**G** 204	
B 255		**B** 204		**B** 153		**B** 102		**B** 51		**B** 0	
# FFCCFF		**#** FFCCCC		**#** FFCC99		**#** FFCC66		**#** FFCC33		**#** FFCC00	

216		**215**		**214**		**213**		**212**		**211**	
R 255		**R** 255		**R** 255		**R** 255		**R** 255		**R** 255	
G 255		**G** 255		**G** 255		**G** 255		**G** 255		**G** 255	
B 255		**B** 204		**B** 153		**B** 102		**B** 51		**B** 0	
# FFFFFF		**#** FFFFCC		**#** FFFF99		**#** FFFF66		**#** FFFF33		**#** FFFF00	

Credits

PAGE 4
Unfurled © 1997 MTV and Yahoo! Inc.
Art Directors: Terry Green & Nori-Zso
Tolson
twenty2product

PAGE 5
The PR Hub
Art Director: Darren Campeau,
Campeau Communications

PAGE 6
Artmuseum.net
Creative Director: Tim Barber, Rare
Medium, Designer: Fiel Valdez

PAGE 8
© 1995 Total Entertainment Network, Inc.
Art Directors: Terry Green & Nori-Zso
Tolson
twenty2product

PAGE 10
National Coffee Brands, Inc.
Art Director: Nina Dietzel
300 Feet Out, Designers: Anahi Carillo,
Anna Bervander, Bret Hansen

PAGE 12
RockShox © 1999 RockShox
Art Directors: Terry Green & Nori-Zso
Tolson
twenty2product

PAGE 12
Shift © 1999 twenty2product and
Daniel Jenett
Art Directors: Terry Green & Nori-Zso
Tolson
twenty2product, Daniel Jenett

PAGE 13
Fox Interactive
Creative Director: Tim Barber, Rare
Medium, Designers: George Rodgers,
Fiel Valdez

PAGE 16
© 2000 DigiScents
Art Directors: Terry Green & Nori-Zso
Tolson
twenty2product

PAGE 17
© altpick.com
Art Director: John Caserta

PAGE 20
© Grande Vitesse.
Art Director: Nina Dietzel
300 Feet Out, Designer: Dava
Guthmiller

PAGE 22
© 1997 Hewlett-Packard Company
Art Directors: Terry Green & Nori-Zso
Tolson
twenty2product

PAGE 23
© 1997 MTV and Yahoo! Inc.
Art Directors: Terry Green & Nori-Zso
Tolson
twenty2product

PAGE 23
© Deloitte Holt
Design: DNA Visual Business Solutions

PAGE 24
© Ameritech
Design: DNA Visual Business Solutions

PAGE 24
© Xuma
Art Director: Nina Dietzel
300 Feet Out, Designer: David
Guthmiller

PAGE 25
© Federal Express
Design: DNA Visual Business Solutions

PAGES 26–27
Absinthe
Art Director: Nina Dietzel, 300 Feet Out,
Designer: Ryan Medeiros

PAGE 28
Casino Royale
Art Director: Mark Wyman, Delf Design

PAGE 34
West African Highlife
Art Director: Joshua Jacobson,
Jdesign.com

PAGE 35
Atlas Magazine
Art Director: Amy Franceschini,
Futurefarmers, Editor: Olivier Laude,
Programmer: Michael Macrone

PAGE 36
Kotoja
Art Director: Joshua Jacobson,
Jdesign.com

PAGE 42
Savvio
Art Director: Nina Dietzel, 300 Feet Out,
Designer: Anna Bervander

PAGES 43–44
Neiman Marcus
Creative Director: Tim Barber, Rare
Medium, Designers: Fiel Valdez, George
Rodgers

PAGE 50
Invivo
Logo created by Energy Energy Design,
web site created by Webb Design
Art Director: Vaughn Shields, Webb
Design, Designer: Hallvard Nakken

PAGES 51–52
Terrascope
Art Directors: Bill Dunlap & Steve
Bishop, Terrascope.

PAGE 58
Color Paramount
Designer: Lane Good, Fast Lane Studios

PAGES 59–60
Lumina
© 1998 Lane Hall Productions and NEC
Art Directors: Terry Green & Nori-Zso
Tolson
twenty2product

PAGES 66–68
Britney Spears
Creative Director: Karen Shields, DNA
Visual Business Solutions, Web
Designer: Jessica Schnepf

PAGES 74–75
Venus Sports
Art Director: Nina Dietzel, 300 Feet Out,
Designer: Anna Bervander

PAGE 76
Xpedior
Web Engineering: Mark Gunson, Project
Director: Stephen Liem, Strategy and
Design: Chip Taylor, Xpedior

PAGE 82
Fast Lane Studios
Designer: Lane Good, Fast Lane Studios

PAGE 83
Seascapes
Creative Designer: Frank Amodo,
RevaComm

PAGE 84
Futurefarmers
Concept and Design: Amy Franceschini,
Futurefarmers, Contributing
Programmers: Sacha Merg, Justin Bakse,
Josh On, Michael Macrone,
Contributing Artists: Sacha Merg,
Keitra Dixon, Stella Lai

PAGE 90
Artmuseum.net
Creative Director: Tim Barber, Rare
Medium, Designer: Fiel Valdez

PAGES 91–92
Dell
© 1999 Atmark (Japan) and Dell
Computer Inc. Art Directors: Terry Green
& Nori-Zso Tolson
twenty2product

PAGE 98
Fox Interactive
Creative Director: Tim Barber, Rare
Medium, Designers: George Rodgers,
Fiel Valdez

PAGES 99–100
Unfurled
© 1997 MTV and Yahoo! Inc. Art
Directors: Terry Green & Nori-Zso Tolson
twenty2product

PAGE 106
Altpick
© altpick.com.
Art Director: John Caserta

PAGE 107
PFA-Architects
Planning, Design, and Development:
Chip Taylor, M8BIUS Intermedia

PAGE 108
Cymatix
Art Director: Darren Campeau,
Campeau Communications

PAGES 114–115
Smith and Hawken Teak
Art Director: Vaughn Shields, Webb
Design, Design: Hallvard Nakken
Smith and Hawken feature:
Art Director: Vaughn Shields, Webb
Design, Design: Matt Bolen

PAGE 116
Intel MediaDome
Creative Director: Tim Barber, Rare
Medium, Designer: Paul Lee

PAGE 122
Decision-Dynamix
Designer: Joshua Jacobson, Agency:
OMIX, Inc.

PAGES 123–124
RockShox
© 1999 RockShox
Art Directors: Terry Green & Nori-Zso
Tolson
twenty2product

PAGE 130
discussions.com
Art Directors: Bill Dunlap and Steve
Bishop, Terrascope

PAGES 131–132
MCI Corporate Store
Designer: Joshua Jacobson, Agency:
OMIX, Inc.

PAGES 138–139
DNA
Creative Director: Karen Shields, DNA
Visual Business Solutions, Designers:
Jessica Schnepf, Dru Jennett

PAGE 140
RevaComm
Creative Design: Todd Masui, RevaComm

PAGE 146
uRreal
Art Director: Luke Desantos, uRreal

PAGES 147–148
Commerce One
© 1999 Commerce One.
Art Directors: Terry Green & Nori-Zso
Tolson
twenty2product

PAGE 154
The PR Hub
Art Director: Darren Campeau,
Campeau Communications

PAGE 155
Race for the Cure
Design: Hallvard Nakken, Agency:
Webb Design

PAGE 156
Giftemporia.com
Art Director: Nina Dietzel, 300 Feet Out,
Designer: Kha Hoang

PAGE 162
Digiscents
© 2000 DigiScents, Art Directors: Terry
Green & Nori-Zso Tolson
twenty2product

PAGE 163
Hawaii International Film Fest
Creative Team: Steven Tu, Frank Amodo,
Wilson Wong, RevaComm

PAGE 164
Chefwear
Creative Director: Karen Shields, DNA
Visual Business Solutions, Web
Designer: Jessica Schnepf

PAGE 170
RockShox
© 1999 RockShox
Art Directors: Terry Green & Nori-Zso
Tolson
twenty2product

PAGE 171
© Lily Fighera Hats
Art Director: Nina Dietzel
Designer: Shiro Hamamoto
300 Feet Out

PAGE 172
RockShox
© 1999 RockShox
Art Directors: Terry Green & Nori-Zso
Tolson
twenty2product

PAGE 173
© 1995 Total Entertainment Network, Inc.
Art Directors: Terry Green & Nori-Zso
Tolson
twenty2product

PAGE 173
© 2000 DigiScents
Art Directors: Terry Green & Nori-Zso
Tolson
twenty2product

Directory

Tim Barber
Creative Director
Rare Medium
164 Townsend Street, #4
San Francisco CA 94107
(415) 957-1975
fax: (415) 957-1976
email: timb@raremedium.com

Darren Campeau
Art Director
Campeau Communications
1651 Fulton Street
San Francisco, CA 94117
(415) 775-4457
fax: (415) 775-4456
email: d@dcampeau.com

John Caserta
Visual Communications Expert
69 Valley Street
San Francisco, CA 94110
(415) 254-5060
http://johncaserta.com

Luke Desantos
Creative Director
uRreal Inc.
990 Linden Drive, Suite 201
Santa Clara, CA 95050
(408) 248-9151
fax: (408) 248-9299
email: luke@uRreal.com

Janina Dietzel
Creative Director
300 Feet Out
Pier 9, Suite 114
The Embarcadero
San Francisco, CA 94111
(415) 477-9940, ext. 12
fax: (415) 477-9946
email: nina_d@300feetout.com

Bill Dunlap
Art Director
Terrascope
54 Mint Street, Suite 110
San Francisco, CA 94103
(415) 951-4944
fax: (415) 625-0306
email: bill@terrascope.com

Amy Franceschini
Founder, 1995
Futurefarmers
1201 Howard Street, Suite B
San Francisco, CA 94103
(415) 552-2124
fax: (415) 626-8953
email: ame@sirius.com

Lane Good
Creative Director
Fast Lane Studios
290 Larkspur Plaza Drive
Larkspur, CA 94939
(415) 637-4149
fax: (888) 392-4832 ext. 415-927-4130
email: lane@fastlanestudios.com

Terry Green & Nori-Zso Tolson
Partners
twenty2product
440 Davis Court, #509
San Francisco, CA 94114-2412
(415) 399-9744
fax: (415) 399-9622
email: info@twenty2.com

Joshua Jacobson
Jdesign.com
977 Fell Street
San Francisco, CA 94117
email: jmania@alumni.stanford.org

Karen Shields
Creative Director
DNA Visual Business Solutions
212 West Superior, Suite 400
Chicago, IL 60610
(312) 654-8383 ext. 22
fax: (312) 654-8388
www.dnavbs.com

Vaughn Shields
Creative Director
Webb Design
Pier 50 at 401 China Basin
Suite 126
San Francisco, CA 94107
(415) 546-7707
fax: (415) 546-4004
email: vaughn@webbdesign.com

Chip Taylor
Executive Producer
M8BIUS Intermedia
email: ctaylor@m8bius.com
and
Creative Manager
Xpedior
44 Montgomery Street, Suite 3200
San Francisco, CA 94104
(415) 399-7287
fax: (415) 399-7001
email: chip.taylor@xpedior.com

Gena Uehara
Marketing Director
RevaComm
700 Bishop Street, Suite 401
Honolulu, HI 96813
(808) 599-8872
fax: (808) 599-8905
email: guehara@revacomm.com

Mark Wyman
Web Designer
Delf Design
317A Eureka Street
San Francisco, CA 94114
(415) 826-6674
email: harmonk@sirius.com